Lincoln Christian

P9-CPY-095

Preaching About Life
in a Threatening World

Preaching About ... Series

Preaching About Life in a Threatening World

Ronald J. Sider and Michael A. King

The Westminster Press
Philadelphia

© 1987 Ronald J. Sider and Michael A. King

All rights reserved—no part of this book may be reproduced in any form without permission in writing from the publisher, except by a reviewer who wishes to quote brief passages in connection with a review in magazine or newspaper.

Scripture quotations from the Revised Standard Version of the Bible are copyrighted 1946, 1952, © 1971, 1973 by the Division of Christian Education of the National Council of the Churches of Christ in the U.S.A. and are used by permission.

Grateful acknowledgment is made to the following for permission to quote from copyrighted works:

The Christian Century for quotations from "Feminism and Peace" by Rosemary Radford Ruether, from the August 31–September 7, 1983, issue. Copyright 1983 Christian Century Foundation.

Minnesota Public Radio, St. Paul, Minnesota, for quotations from "Letter from Jim" by Garrison Keillor, *News from Lake Wobegon: Original Monologues,* Spring 1983 (cassette tape).

Book design by Christine Schueler

First edition

Published by The Westminster Press®
Philadelphia, Pennsylvania

PRINTED IN THE UNITED STATES OF AMERICA

9 8 7 6 5 4 3 2 1

Library of Congress Cataloging-in-Publication Data

Sider, Ronald J.
   Preaching about life in a threatening world.

   (Preaching about— series)
   Bibliography: p.
   1. Preaching.   2. Christianity and politics.
3. Christianity and justice.   4. Peace—Religious
aspects—Christianity.   5. Church and the world.
I. King, Michael A.   II. Title.   III. Series.
BV4235.P7S35   1987   251   87–8179
ISBN 0–664–24082–8 (pbk.)

Contents

Preface and Acknowledgments   7

1 Peace, Justice, and Fairy Tales   9

2 Story and the Dimensions of the Issues   29

3 The Biblical Story's Perspective on Key Issues   53

4 Building a Biblical House of Being   74

5 Social Justice Preaching: Some Nuts and Bolts   93

6 From Ivory Tower to Life in the Story   108

Appendix: Finding Information on the Issues   117

Notes   121

Bibliography   129

28 Ma 88

77058

Preface and Acknowledgments

Those who are familiar, from previous writings, with both of the authors' individual styles may well wonder whether Ron's style underwent a massive metamorphosis or Mike did most of the writing. Without excluding the possibility or desirability of the former, we would encourage the reader to operate with the second hypothesis.

We would like to thank those wonderful people without whom this book could not have been written:

Our wives, Arbutus Lichti Sider and Joan Kenerson King, for putting up with and supporting us during our periods of writer's insanity.

Our congregations, Diamond Street Mennonite Church and Germantown Mennonite Church, for being the laboratories in which many of the ideas in this book were tested.

And Phil Weber and Phyllis Krabill, whose sacrificial lending of their computer transformed the mechanics of writing from horror into pleasant drudgery.

1

Peace, Justice, and Fairy Tales

We approach the pulpit, we preachers, with our frailties and our insecurities and our wistful hope that *this* time it will work, this time someone will care about what we have to say. In our dreams, the congregants lean forward, their eyes searching for new truth, their ears ready to take in any wisp of wisdom. In reality, a trace of expectancy quivers on the faces of the dwellers in the pews: just a trace. Once in a while full-fledged interest flares. More often, even that last trace winks out. Pews creak as bodies twist and slump their way down into comfort.

What has gone wrong? we wonder, as we ourselves now slump before a Sunday lunch turned tasteless by defeat. Why won't they listen to our proclamations of liberty to the captives and recovery of sight for the blind? We preach about national and international concerns. We preach about the interlocking destinies of the poor and the rich, of the oppressed and the oppressing, of humans, animals, trees, and the great blue seas. We preach about the very fate of the earth and its inhabitants. Yet still they slump.

Why? And what would change the slumping figures to bodies straining forward? This book will not claim to answer definitively questions such as these; of the writing of books on preaching, and of their authors' claims to provide surefire ways to energize preaching, there is no end. Nevertheless, we want to wrestle with some possible causes, and suggest some potential antidotes, for the malaise by which preaching often seems afflicted.

In succeeding chapters we will spell out in more detail the

implications of our approach and the way it affects the nuts and bolts of preaching. Though much of what we say is applicable to preaching in general, we will be keeping in mind our primary focus: preaching about national and international concerns—the large, often global, concerns of our era and the issues of justice, peace, and freedom that are inextricably intertwined with them.

A long list of possible reasons for the slumping in the pews could be given. Perhaps the preaching is too judgmental. The preacher, like the heroes in old Greek plays, yields to hubris, to overweening pride, and so, becoming as God, calls the sinners in the pews to account for their misdeeds. Perhaps the preaching is too abstract. Many golden words about the heavenly sweetness of life in the kingdom of God spew forth, but how one lives at the same time in God's kingdom and in the real world never quite becomes clear. Perhaps the preaching is too woodenly biblical. The Bible becomes an impressive old historic house; the preacher, turned tour guide, forces the tired tourists to inspect every architectural detail and listen to each interminable story about the bullets that made those holes. Perhaps the preaching is too worldly. The preacher cares not a whit about that grand old mansion which is the Bible and within whose grandeur those who care to enter can still dwell; wanting to build a modern house, the preacher never notices that two-inch plastic moldings suffer when compared with the seven or eight inches of ornately carved beauty the Bible uses to edge its walls.

We could go on, expounding upon ways such weaknesses in preaching can kill the last vestige of expectancy. But before the weaknesses can be explored, two fundamental and interrelated problems—*numbed parishioners* and *opaque preaching*—need to be examined.

Numbed Parishioners

Al Krass has some insightful things to say about what may cause parishioners to slump even when the preacher feels the word has been preached with fiery enthusiasm. It's not that they just don't care, says Krass, it's that they care too much; they are numbed by fear of all the structures that may be coming unglued or are glued together in ways that perpetuate evil. It's that they care so much—as the terrorist bullets fly and the farms fail and the tropical rain forests give way to slash-and-burn and the sky threatens to flare with a glow not the sun's—that they dare not approach the shores of the ocean of internal feeling which is their caring. If they did, they might fall in and drown. Krass mentions psychologist Robert Jay Lifton, who worked with survivors of Hiroshima, and suggests that we, like the Japanese when faced with a world filled with actualities and possibilities too frightening to bear, repress our feelings. We are afflicted by "psychic numbing."[1]

Krass also quotes Joanna Rogers Macy, who says the numbness, the seeming apathy, "is born not out of callousness, but out of confusion about how to accept and deal with our pain for the world."[2] If indeed this is the case, then at least to some extent the slumps of our parishioners are to be interpreted not as signals of apathy but as signals of an ocean of fear and rage and of tears barely suppressed. It may be that out there in the pews toss dark and stormy seas. If those seas were acknowledged and their existence owned, they could be transformed. If each numbed Christian were touched at the right depth, the fury of those suppressed waters could be released in waves of passion to transform the world.

Opaque vs. Transparent Preaching: Content

If such seas do exist, how might they be tapped? The answer to that question leads us to an examination of the second fundamental problem, the problem of opaque preaching. Much contemporary preaching is weak because it is *opaque,* when what it most desperately needs is to be *transparent*—to the transcendent, the sacred, the divine. Other ways of putting it might be that much preaching remains mired in the immanent, this-worldly, purely historical or profane dimension of existence.

Opaque Preaching

Opaque preaching suffers from a closed quality. This existence, this reality, this history, these lives we have been handed are all we have to reckon with. If the world is about to burn with nuclear flames and drown in toxic wastes and be slashed by mounting crime, and if the horsemen of the apocalypse appear to be thundering across the earth too fast and furiously to be caught, there is nothing to be done about it but to make the best of a bad situation. And there is nothing more powerful than such forces to fill us with the hope that we may in some way overcome them. There is no transcendent reality, no God larger than and sovereign over history, no God whose powerful yet gentle presence can give us the courage to face and unleash the power of the oceans of suppressed feeling surging within each human self.

This opaque, closed quality is not present in all preaching, of course. There is some perfectly good transparent preaching being done. In some traditions transparency to the divine is even so highly valued as to be overvalued. It is perhaps precisely that overvaluing in the fundamentalist or evangelical roots many of us possess that has led to the current opacity from which much of our preaching suffers. For many generations we have been baking pie in the sky. Now we are ready to bring the pies back down and eat some good slices right here on earth.

This has been a needed reaction, this determination to link Christianity with the concrete, pressing issues of the day. As countless articulate voices from the realm of black, liberation, feminist, and other theologies have been telling us, salvation is not just a spiritual or otherworldly reality. It has radical implications for this real and desperate world, a world in which the poor and hungry and tortured need more than salvation from their personal sin, though they need that too.

Some, however, have not been satisfied to reclaim immanence as one dimension of the gospel. They have been so suspicious of the ethereal Christianity which a concern for transcendence sometimes promotes that they have tended to reject transcendence entirely. Liberation theologians occasionally fall into this camp—regrettably but understandably, since their thinking grows out of oppressive contexts in which the failures of heaven-bound, apolitical theologies are all too evident.

José Miranda, for example, seems to want salvation to incorporate only this-worldly, immanent, nontranscendent aspects. God, the author of our salvation, is not to be sought outside the stream of history but is to be discovered within it. "To know Yahweh is to achieve justice for the poor," says Miranda.[3] He adds, "The God who does not allow himself to be objectified, because only in the immediate command of conscience is he God, clearly specifies that he is knowable *exclusively* in the cry of the poor and the weak who seek justice."[4] If one thinks God's existence and functioning *is* limited to that which is worked out in history, one can argue that Miranda's view retains some transparency to the divine. But if God actually transcends history, though remaining active and visible within it, then Miranda's view is an opaque one.

Such opacity afflicts much of current preaching that wrestles with issues of social justice. Once it was granted, and validly so, that God's kingdom had practical implications for our economic, social, and political lives, it became easier and easier to be seduced into believing that the kingdom functions *only* at that level. Preaching limited to that level suffers from the deficiency Hauerwas and Willimon believe they see in the church as a whole: "It is simply atheistic." It is, to quote the title of an article they have written on the topic, "embarrassed by God's presence."[5]

Yes, we preach good news to the captives and recovery of sight to the blind, but to the extent that it is our good news rather than God's good news, we do in fact, though we would never willingly admit it, preach as atheists. History, in its customary workings, has brought bad news to millions, perhaps billions, of lives. Does one offer such sufferers any really good news, anything much greater than functional atheism, if one preaches to them that the same historical processes that brought them sadness in the first place can now be trusted to bring salvation?

Mircea Eliade might say such preaching is *profane*. What is true of profane persons, or "modern nonreligious man" (Eliade was writing in sexist times), is true of the preacher who regards herself or himself "solely as the subject and agent of history, and . . . refuses all appeal to transcendence. In other words, he accepts no model for humanity outside the human condition as it can be seen in the various historical situations."[6]

The profane preacher of sermons about national or global concerns is the one who skillfully dissects the ways in which hunger in whatever country is currently in the news is caused by economic structures that favor the rich over the poor nations—and then suggests, as the *only* solution to such troubles, a series of responses at the same level as the troubles. Boycott the offending corporations. Lobby national governments to set up more equitable structures. Where is God? What *is* such preaching if not atheistic in practice? God may be invoked somewhere in the sermon, perhaps as the inspiration behind the thoughts of the Amos upon whose cries for justice the sermon is founded, but God is not much seen as an ingredient in the new world the sermon envisions.

Transparent Preaching

Opacity. Profanity. Embarrassment before God. What are the antidotes? What might it mean for preaching to become transparent to the transcendent, the sacred, the divine? Part of the answer might be for us preachers to acknowledge the limits of pie-in-the-sky theology without rejecting its strengths. We could acknowledge the embarrassing limitations of theologies that encouraged missionaries to walk among people whose bodies were starving, whose dignity racism was slaughtering, and worry only about the condition of their immortal souls. We could acknowledge such limitations without at the same time jettisoning the passion of such theologies nourished by faith in a living God, a God more than the sum total of the processes of history. Hauerwas and Willimon speak of such a God when they say:

> At last, we lay our theological cards on the table. We believe . . . that God has acted in Israel and in Jesus, and continues to act in the church today, transforming the world. Our Sunday worship is immoral and indifferent (if not rather silly), unless we really believe that God is present in our gathering and in the world, and that our listening to the story, our service to others and our breaking of bread are dangerous attempts to let God be God.[7]

A. James Reimer criticizes tendencies toward opacity within his own Mennonite tradition. He argues against the excessive historicization of existence that characterizes views like Miranda's, which he believes are influenced by secular perspectives fed by the Enlightenment. In the Enlightenment understanding, God is largely, if not fully, equated with history.

Reimer rightly insists that biblical faith, on the other hand, "presupposed an absolutely transcendent spiritual reality (God), a presupposition which is lacking in the modern historicist view."[8] God is larger than those dark forces of history causing so many to retreat into their ocean of inner numbness. The preacher who operates from this point of view is on the way to transparency.

Eliade might see such a preacher as moving beyond profanity to appreciation of the sacred. Openness to the sacred, a characteristic of Eliade's "religious" person as well as of transparent preaching, is openness to some sort of reality that is higher or deeper or larger than the world but that manifests itself in the world.[9]

To the extent that we preachers can accept such transparency, our preaching will offer more comfort than the evanescent assurance that the kingdom will *someday* fully come for those fortunate enough to be alive at the right time. It will burn with the flames of the living God. It will throb with the good news that release of the captives and recovery of sight for the blind come ultimately—though certainly not in the absence of our faithful efforts—only because our very God still lives and is their guarantor.

Opaque vs. Transparent Preaching: Form

What happens when transparent preaching is actually tried? It was, in fact, once tried by one of us in a sermon called "Their Haunting Secret." That sermon attempted to convey much of what we have examined in the preceding section. It began by telling of unidentified church members haunted by a secret. Their secret is that even as they "outwardly live their lives of faith," even as they "reach out to the heavens with hungry, pleading hands, wanting to be grasped by something other than themselves, wanting to

tremble before an awesome and mysterious presence"—
even as they do all that—"inside they know only that they
are unsure of what they hope for and uncertain of what they
do not see."[10]

Yes, one summer day in which heat and humidity reached
awesome proportions, that sermon was taken into a pulpit
and preached. In all its transparent power and glory it was
preached, and pew after pew should have been lightened of
its load as its dwellers, pierced to the quick by this exposure
of their haunting secret, leaned forward, their eyes reveal-
ing their longing for a healing of their wound.

That is what should have happened, but should and did
are not the same. There were, yes, a few with eyes
transfixed. But there were many more who stared with eyes
glazed by boredom. Why? Could it be that transparent
preaching is just one more gimmick to be sampled, then
forgotten? It *could* well be.

But we would not be exploring so intently the potential
of transparent preaching if we didn't think it existed, so
what might be some other reasons for the underwhelming
response stimulated by the sermon? It is hard to know for
sure. Weather, the blowing where it will of the Spirit's wind,
the secret needs of congregants, all affect a sermon. Sometimes there simply are no clear reasons for a sermon's suc-
cess or failure to be found. Who can really say why it is that
some sermons soar into the heavens without effort while
others never get the millstone off their neck? Who can say
why the soarers sometimes are the ones that look like clunk-
ers in the study while the ones that leap and dance in private
wilt into wallflowers and shrink into a corner the instant
they enter the pulpit?

Who can say? But before we yield entirely to such mystery
and bring this book to an abrupt end, we want to do a bit
more theorizing. "Their Haunting Secret" was an attempt
at transparent preaching. But it was, as it turns out upon
closer examination, a limited attempt. Its *content* was transparent, but its *form* was considerably more opaque. It wrestled tolerably well with the *idea* of transparency but con-
veyed the *experience* of transparency less ably, as it moved
past its anecdotal beginning to a relatively philosophical
discussion of the issues. That there may be something
worth exploring here is borne out by the fact that those few

who did lean forward in their pews were the thinkers, the philosophers, people stimulated by ideas.

Opaque Form: Propositional

The rest, however, performed their slumping act again. They may have done so because this sermon was an example of what Richard Jensen calls "didactic" preaching. Such preaching is rooted in the "Gutenberg galaxy," that world created by the confluence of Gutenberg's printing press; the Enlightenment emphasis on reason, order, logic, science; and the consequent favoring of logical, analytical, propositional ways of processing truth.

Didactic preaching is characterized by marks such as these:

Teaching the biblical text in question becomes the goal.

The points to be made in the process of this teaching are then drawn from the text—even when the text is not didactic in nature (and only a minority of texts are didactic).

These points are presented in orderly, systematic fashion.

The desired response to the sermon is assent to the ideas as true.

The whole aim of the sermon is to appeal to the hearer's *intellect.* [11]

"Their Haunting Secret" probably fits into the category of didactic preaching. Though attempts were made to present the ideas in it as interestingly as possible, the realm of ideas controlled it. Was its weakness, then—and an underlying cause for the boredom it produced in many—that in its form it was opaque, profane, embarrassed by God's presence? Eugene L. Lowry believes that much of what is wrong with contemporary preaching is that it majors in organizing ideas rather than shaping experience.[12] It tries to chop the Bible or God or human experience into logically identified bits and pieces, which are then reorganized into whatever the preacher considers the most valid form—often a sermon with an introduction, three points, and a conclusion.

That approach is not entirely bad; we were, after all, created with intellects that provide us with key tools for taking in, evaluating, organizing, and acting out truth. But it can easily work at cross-purposes with what the preacher is actually trying to achieve, which includes the creation of a space into which the divine can flow. There is in such preaching, argues Lowry, "the problem of control. The image of ordering ideas assumes a resultant mastery. One gets the truth in place, declares it, puts it into a proposition. Putty in one's hands. The matter is closed—even if the preacher does not intend such a result."[13]

To the extent that Lowry is correct, such preaching risks functional atheism. It risks hubris in its implicit belief that it can wrestle God's truth into submission to three clear points. It risks opacity to the divine in its dependence on a form biased toward a nice, neat coherence, which in its very neatness may shut out the majestic raggedness with which the divine often shatters orderly preconceptions.

Again, the argument here is not for some sort of thoroughgoing anti-intellectualism. Intellectually derived propositions can serve, at the right time, as clear and coherent summaries of the larger truth they can never fully capture. The proposition presented in "Their Haunting Secret," the idea that the Greek/Platonic and Hebrew ways of viewing life can be partially integrated rather than being forever utterly dichotomized is worth exploring. The problem is that the preaching moment is often the wrong time and the wrong place to do it. The *right* moment is probably the *teaching* moment. It is in the classroom that the most propositional, didactic methods of processing life belong. Teaching, after all, is the meaning lying at the heart of the word "didactic."

If the preaching moment is not primarily the teaching moment (though teaching need not be expelled from but only submit to the sermon's larger purpose), then what is it? It is the time and place to call into life the power throbbing in a story, the biblical story, which is not couched just in "propositional truths about God, for that would appeal only to our intellects, ignoring the biblical happenings and giving us no way to live into them."[14]

Transparent Form: Story

At last we get to the heart of the matter: story. It is the absence of story that makes so much preaching opaque. Preaching without story lends itself to the human endeavor to close the cracks that the divine needs to creep into our lives. Story is riddled with cracks. Story opens up, leads onward and upward and into adventure, into larger and larger meanings without end; story at last brings all but the most jaded to the edge of their seats, because with story you can never be quite sure what will come next, as the plot unfolds and the tension mounts and the outcome remains in doubt.

It was probably the submission of story to idea that defeated "Their Haunting Secret." It began on a note of story, the story of those haunted by a secret. As long as that note was maintained, interest tagged along. But as soon as the sermon moved into its main theme, attempting through the sharing of ideas to explain the causes of the haunting secret, listeners lost interest if they didn't happen to care about that particular set of ideas. If some way had been found to present the same material without losing the story element—such as by telling from beginning to end the story of someone plagued by the haunting secret, then healed by an experience of transcendence—interest might have been maintained.

But story gave way to proposition. And proposition summarizes, closes down, tidies up, seals cracks. Certainly propositions can be communicated interestingly and with some degree of open-endedness. In a later chapter we will suggest ways this can happen. Nevertheless, propositions aim much more toward closure than does story. The most valued idea is apt to be the most clearly expressed idea, the one leaving the least uncertainty in the recipient's mind as to the meaning its articulator intends to convey. For that reason, propositions, to put it bluntly, have a good chance of boring; story has a good chance of fascinating.

This brings to mind the movie *Out of Africa*, which tells the story of the years that writer Karen Blixen (pen name Isak Dinesen) spent in Africa, and of her relationships first with her husband and then, when the marriage soured, with

Denys Finch-Hatton. That story could be boiled down into propositions, accurate summaries of the facts and details of one woman's life: The year she went to Africa. The year she left. The number of rooms in her house and the number of servants in the rooms. How much coffee she grew in which growing season. Such details were, in fact, not entirely irrelevant to the story, just as propositions should not be entirely irrelevant to the sermon.

What made the movie powerful, however, had little to do with the details and almost everything to do with the story. Gradually it builds, this tale of a woman who starts out by yelling "Shoo!" at African natives as if they were chickens and lives in a nice European mansion that looks as if it ended up on the African landscape through an accidental warp in the space-time continuum. Little by little she begins to settle into Africa and into a growing respect for the heritage of the black tribespeople, with whom she builds a relationship larger than "Shoo!" She meets and begins to love Denys, who loves and blends with the beauty that is Africa. There are moments of tenderness and passion; there is the table set for two out in the middle of nowhere as night falls over the wild land and they sit and share talk, food, silence, and the land; there is the heartbreak as relationships with land and people break.

By its end the movie has achieved something a stark propositional summary never could have. The watcher is in tears, and this tale of long-dead people in a distant land roars within like the lions who pace over the grave of a loved one at the movie's end. Yet it is never entirely clear to the watcher precisely what it is that causes tears and awe to throb. One knows that somehow one has been touched and moved and perhaps even forever changed and bettered, but one is not quite sure why. One only knows what has happened, without having the power to squeeze it into a handful of nicely articulated propositions.

That is what story can do, and that is what a sermon sensitive to the power of story can and should do. It should leave behind in the hearer a trembling of tears and a tingling of spines and at the center a mystery called God. It should do so, however, not just because thus will interest be gained and thus can the preacher go home to Sunday lunch feeling happy and hungry. It should do so above all else because the business of preaching is the sharing of the Bible, and the business of the Bible is at heart the sharing of a wild and wonderful Story.

When that dimension is allowed to charge our preaching, then at last it can be transparent, open to the sacred and unembarrassed by God's presence and therefore gripping. Then at last can the good news bubble forth, the good news that we are all living out a Story that is taking place right here and now on earth. But it is a Story told by a storyteller larger than any that earth can provide, a Story therefore not limited to the confines of earthly reality. It is a Story larger than life though rooted within life, and therefore a Story that holds out genuine hope, even to the mother in Ethiopia cradling her dead child and to the Soviet dissident recoiling from the dead Siberian winter.

Preaching about social issues, about national and international concerns—preaching that is placed in such a context is preaching with true power to change the world precisely because it knows that not it but the God whose spirit breathes through it will do the changing. It is preaching that has healed the wound splitting reality into two totally separated realms: transcendent and immanent, sacred and profane, spiritual and actual, otherworldly and this-worldly. It is pie-in-the-sky preaching that has learned to share the taste, though not the whole of the pie, with those not yet in the sky.

It is preaching that first of all is *biblical* and, second, opens itself to a realm not normally associated with hard-headed preaching about social justice—the realm of *fairy tale.* It is biblical because the healing of the wound is precisely what the Bible cares passionately about.

The Biblical Story

In the beginning God broods over the deep. Then God begins to tell a Story. From the brooding breaks forth good creation, and for a brief spell it seems the Story has begun and, almost in the same breath, ended happily. Soon, however, creation offered to humanity as beautiful gift falls. Humanity takes the gift freely offered and tries to turn it into possession.

Rupture is not the end of the story, however, only the beginning of a new and torturous phase: the beginning of the long road forward to a restored creation. God continues to tell the Story. God calls forth from among the men and women broken by the fall a chosen people. They will become characters in the Story, and they will know, more clearly than any characters have known before, that a Story is being told, and that they are called to live it out as a light and a guide for all people. God makes a covenant with the people to continue to tell the Story. And here, given our concerns, comes the crucial point: this is a covenant made by a God whose being transcends the realm of space and time; it is also a covenant that "cannot be understood without real hope for its embodiment of Shalom in time and space."[15]

In time and space, shalom is embodied indeed. The covenant is embodied in the exodus, that event in which the roar of a mighty God so tangibly makes history shudder; that event in which a people leave behind palpable, physical, earthly oppression in an equally palpable journey toward an earthly Promised Land. But that event, in the telling of those who remembered it over the centuries, would cease to be meaningful if the role of the Storyteller were left out. And if any credence is to be given to the biblical witness—with its attestations of wonderful coincidences and awesome serendipities in the confluence of such forces as wind and water to make passable land not normally so—without God the event itself would not have been.

After the wonderful turn in the Story that was the exodus, there happened what seems to happen often after such turns. The chosen people wandered away from their covenant with God, their commitment to obey the law God had given them as a guide to how they were to live if their new land was indeed to be the Promised Land.[16] Then, and over and over again throughout their history, they had to be called back to the Story that God was trying to tell through their lives. They had to be called back, for example, by the prophets who rose up to mediate the Story, the prophets who yearned for, pleaded for, and demanded the fulfillment of the Story. Forever—so potent are those ancient images—will the prophetic sword-turned-plowshare plow the fields of the Lord; forever past the banks of those fields in God's country, watering and cooling them, will flow the waters of justice and righteousness.

In God's country, God's kingdom, cry the prophets, there will be peace and freedom; the ruptured fabric will be knit. Within nature peace will reign. And between humans and nature. Between humans. Within humans. But always it is God's country, and God's country is not the utopia of human efforts triumphant at last, but the country we enter when at last the most awful rupture is healed and we make, at all the levels of our existence, our peace with God. Always this Story of our movement toward the divine country is inseparable from the fact that it is indeed a Story being told, moved, shaped by a teller, without whom it would cease to exist.

Then, exploding into the middle of the Story, comes the news that the teller has decided to play a double role. The teller has decided to become one of us, a character in the Story, a human being. The teller has decided not only to direct the Story but to be buffeted by the Story from within, and so to make much clearer than ever before just where the Story is headed and what it will take to get there. Jesus comes on the scene, and Jesus models for us muddled characters the kind of living that will bring about the joyful climax the teller has in mind. Jesus offers, as Fackre puts it, "miracles of shalom," forgiving sinners, healing the sick and the cynical, raising the dead.[17]

This Jesus, human being that he was, modeled for us the kind of living it takes to bring about shalom. But a good deal of what Jesus modeled was known to contribute to shalom long before he came along; the problem was that knowing and doing remained two different things. This is not the place to go into complex debates about the nature of Jesus, but the mystery of his divinity, though mystery indeed, is a crucial part of the Story. Because Jesus was human, he provided a tangible example for us to follow. But because he was divine, in providing that example faithfully to the death and beyond, his atoning work healed the rupture between us characters and our Storyteller to the extent that we now not only know where our Story is heading but possess power to live it out.[18]

When we characters decide to live as Jesus lived and to band together in communities to find strength for the living of the Story in a world that by and large rejects it, we form the church of Christ. We become adventurers moving the

Story forward, finding courage for the way in the faith that the Jesus who most clearly showed the way still lives and waits at journey's end to welcome us into God's country.

We are brought to earth with a thud when we realize that *we* are that band of hardy explorers. We are too much aware of credit card balances that just won't go down. We worry about cracks in some of the joists in the house we own, because if those cracks, God forbid, get much wider, the house is going to fall in. We live in an intractable world where, all this talk of prophets and storytellers notwithstanding, the poor still suffer and the hungry still die. And we who are Christian and rich can't, for the life of us, quite figure out what do with our riches that will make much difference to the poor.

The Christian Story and Fairy Tales

How is that biblical Story ever to break into our lives with power to change them? How are we preachers to share the Story with power, we who live the uneasy lives just described but who must then attempt to offer a message transcending and challenging that uneasiness? That is where *fairy tale* comes in. Fairy tale is a form of story in which anything can happen; the cracks in fairy tales are so wide open as to admit even God. But we speak here of not just any kind of fairy tale but a special kind, the only kind large enough to encompass the glory of the biblical tale. We speak of something J. R. R. Tolkien, a teller of wonderful tales in his own right, spoke of—fairy tale that is both *eucatastrophic* and *true*. First to eucatastrophe (by which Tolkien means *good* catastrophe), then to the true fairy tale:

> The consolation of fairy-stories, the joy of the happy ending: or more correctly of the good catastrophe, the sudden joyous "turn" (for there is no true end to any fairy-tale): this joy, which is one of the things which fairy-stories can produce supremely well, is not essentially "escapist." . . . In its fairy-tale—or otherworldly— setting, it is a sudden and miraculous grace: never to be counted on to recur. It does not deny the existence of *dyscatastrophe*, of sorrow and failure: the possibility of these is necessary to the joy of deliverance; it denies (in the face of much evidence, if you will) universal final

defeat and in so far is *evangelium*, giving a fleeting glimpse of Joy, Joy beyond the walls of the world, poignant as grief.[19]

Tolkien calls this fairy tale—blessed with the sudden, unexpected, joyful turn, the "good" catastrophe—the "eucatastrophic" tale. Surely the biblical Story is such a tale, a tale in which things are constantly going from bad to worse—good creation falls, covenants are abridged, prophets are ignored or mocked—but always there comes the unexpected turn. Creation falls, and God calls forth a wandering Aramean to found a nation. The covenant is abridged, and Hosea, the teller of the eucatastrophic tale, tells of the God who is like a husband who marries a prostitute. The prophets plead, and the rivers of justice dry up; then comes Jesus, offering living water. Jesus dies; then comes the ultimate eucatastrophe.

But the best, according to Tolkien, is yet to come. Not only does the eucatastrophic tale breathe joy but one of them, at least, breathes truth, the truth of being *true:*

> It is not difficult to imagine the peculiar excitement and joy that one would feel, if any specially beautiful fairy-story were found to be "primarily" true, its narrative to be history, without thereby losing the mythical or allegorical significance that it had possessed. It is not difficult, for one is not called upon to try and conceive anything of a quality unknown. The joy would have exactly the same quality . . . as the joy which the "turn" in a fairy-story gives: such joy has the very taste of primary truth. . . . It looks forward (or backward: the direction in this regard is unimportant) to the Great Eucatastrophe. The Christian joy, the *Gloria*, is of the same kind; but it is pre-eminently . . . high and joyous. Because this story is supreme; and it is true. Art has been verified. God is the Lord, of angels, and of men—and of elves. Legend and History have met and fused.[20]

It is that quality which preaching about national and international issues needs and which it so often lacks. It is often thought that when one is preaching about the difficult realities of a difficult world one must stay rigorously rooted in those realities, pointing out the amount of resources consumed by Americans vs. the rest of the world, or the fact that it takes ten pounds of grain to make one pound of beef, so one should eat more grain, less beef. Such realities are not to be avoided, but preaching, while including them, has to rise above them.

To tell a good American how many nuclear warheads are housed in how many silos and how many times over the world can be blown up may be part of helping him or her face current reality. But filling people with images of their many-times-pulverized corpses is a poor goad to action. Being blown up will not, of course, be seen as a pleasant possibility, but it may be seen as inevitable, given the impressive array of numbers with which an attack of sorts has already been launched in the course of the sermon.

Another goad might be the claim that God would be happier with creation and the people in it if the missiles were destroyed. That is no doubt true, and profoundly biblical, but also likely to fall victim to the perceived impossibility of doing much to get rid of the missiles. Such preaching, tragically, may only add to the ocean of repressed feeling instead of offering the hearer a way of tapping the power of such feeling.

"For the sake, as he sees it, of the ones he preaches to," says Frederick Buechner, "the preacher is apt to preach the Gospel with the high magic taken out, the deep mystery reduced to a manageable size."[21] The deep mystery reduced to statistics and secular forces. Ah, but what if, in the midst of all those statistics, it is made clear that we live not in a history merely grinding grimly and mechanically forward, but in the midst of a tale into which eucatastrophe can burst at any time? Buechner says:

> No matter how forgotten and neglected, there is a child in all of us who is not just willing to believe in the possibility that maybe fairy tales are true after all but who is to some degree in touch with that truth. You pull the shade on snow falling, white on white, and the child comes to life for a moment. There is a fragrance in the air, a certain passage of a song, an old photograph falling out from the pages of a book, the sound of somebody's voice in the hall that makes your heart leap and your eyes fill with tears.[22]

"Who can say," Buechner goes on, "when or how it will be that something easters up out of the dimness to remind us of a time before we were born and after we will die?"[23] Who can say—we want those listening to our sermons to ask of themselves—which small act of justice, which letter to Congress, or which bowl of soup fed to a homeless man will be swept up by God into some great joyous turn no one could have envisioned? Always our preaching should breathe of fairy tale, always the cracks should open wider and wider to admit the possibility of divine action. Then, at last, with the sense that every human life is a life that can participate in God's eucatastrophes, each face may turn intently toward the pulpit: not because the preacher is so wonderful, but because what the preacher is mediating—a joy which like a boat could take the sufferer of psychic numbness on a safe voyage across the ocean of tears—is wonderful.

In its very form, especially when touched by fairy-tale overtones, story serves to integrate the transcendent and the immanent, the sacred and the profane. It is able to be transparent to the divine while remaining rooted in the earthly. It can do so because it is simultaneously *linear* and *transparent*. Story possesses, indeed, the kind of Hebraic quality valued by those who rightfully maintain that Christianity must be lived out in history: namely, the power to convey movement, in history, from past to present to future, from beginning through unfolding through fulfillment. But this linearity of story is combined with transparency to mystery, to the unexpected intrusion of forces and actions from beyond.

Story in this combination of linearity and transparency is thus, one could say, an ultimately eschatological form, since eschatology always carries with it a sense of forward movement *and* is usually accompanied by images and hints of a future larger than the ordinary progression of events might lead us to expect. It is a vehicle suited to the conveyance of a faith which holds that history does not move in endless cycles, as many people surrounding the early Israelites thought. It moves forward to a glorious climax (linearity). But it moves not like a clock, wound up long ago and now going on mechanically, but under the direction of a sovereign, transcendent God (transparency).

Such an imposing and propositional word it is—eschatology—yet so accessible when translated into story. Then it becomes simply this: we are all characters in a Story which will, finally, though not without the pain and sorrow and confusion that complicate any powerful story, end in joy; though its ending, the Story being the kind it is, will probably only be a new beginning.

2

Story and the Dimensions of the Issues

Preachers will always be tempted to slice the issues into pieces they can easily understand, explain, and illustrate. That is not all bad; in a world in which any one human being can only grasp tiny parts of a complex whole, all issues have to be simplified in some way if either preachers or listeners are to grasp things that (to paraphrase Job) will always be too wonderful for them to fully understand. Necessary as it is, however, simplification always exacts a toll. Because of it, all preaching to some extent roots itself in a never-never land that only approximates the real world; thus a sermon's vision of the dimensions of a problem and its solution will always be partially illusory.

Though none of us preachers can avoid this simplification and falsification of reality, all of us can grow in our grasp of the world's complexities. As we do so, and as this growth is reflected in our preaching, our sermonic vision will be increasingly true to reality and consequently increasingly powerful. A guide to such growth is what we hope to provide in this chapter. We will do so by committing the sin from which we are trying to be saved: we will suggest ways of taking into account the complexity of reality by simplifying it into four dimensions or levels that the preacher should keep in mind when preaching about an issue. After we have discussed these four dimensions—the transcendent, the structural, the personal, and the interior—we will note the ways story can function to integrate them. Then we will explore the implications of all this for the preaching of the Story. Finally, we will note the role the church plays in the matter.

The Dimensions of the Issues

We have already paid considerable attention to the dimension of *transcendence.* We need only reiterate that the concern here is openness to the divine, to the mysterious, to that which is not easily flattened into scientifically verifiable cause-and-effect relationships.

We have also taken some note of what could be called the *structural* dimension. We dealt with it earlier when discussing those this-worldly aspects of reality which, though they do not exhaust reality, are among its key ingredients. Here we refer to those ways in which the broad social, political, economic, or other forces of history manifest themselves. There is the American free enterprise system, for example, whose dynamics and transactions and patterns combine to form a structure whose shape is sufficiently definite that it can be contrasted with the Soviet centralized economy. To be aware of this dimension is to know that small behaviors or forces or variables cannot be dealt with only in isolation; they must also be viewed in the context of the larger structures in which they exist and which they combine to form.

To understand how NASA decided to launch the doomed space shuttle *Challenger,* one must take into account structural forces. Each little piece of that decision—each engineer's judgments about the safety of the shuttle's booster rockets, the behavior of each person in the chain of command empowered to launch—is important in understanding the whole. But it is not until the whole intricate web of pressures and expectations, the whole structure, comes into focus that the reasons underlying a faulty decision begin to come clear.[1]

At the same time, such structures *are* made up of smaller factors; the decision to launch was made not only by an impersonal structure but also by human beings with faces and names who were asked to account for their decisions. That leads us to a third dimension, the *personal* one. The preacher attempting to deal with this level of the issues will be aware that, at the same time as we all exist within the framework of impersonal structures, such structures also have a personal face. Nazi Germany was swept by forces that transcended the role of any one individual—even Hitler— yet names like Hitler and Hess and Mengele were attached to those forces.

Precisely how, in such a situation, the structural shapes the personal or vice versa (or how any of the dimensions we are discussing affect each other) we are not competent to say—any more than we are able to say precisely to what extent humans are free or determined. Nevertheless, that the dimensions exist and interact seems evident.

A sermon aimed at the personal level (as many are) would focus on the kinds of face-to-face interactions *between* people that make up much of the stuff of everyday life. A sermon that addressed violence by dissecting an altercation between a driver and a gasoline-pump attendant would be so aimed.

A fourth dimension is the *interior* one. Here we are thinking of human subjectivity, of the inward journey, of those aspects of life's adventure that take place inside each person. The preacher who cares about this dimension will care about the fact that people have inner hurts, needs, drives, and dreams that affect how they interact with other dimensions of life. What goes on *within* the driver or the pump attendant is what is at stake here.

Even these four dimensions are a simplification of reality, yet any decent preacher knows that preaching meaningfully about one or two of them is doing a lot. And so the tendency we have already noted in relation to transcendence and immanence—the tendency for the two to be sundered into unrelated parts—is perpetuated in relation to all the dimensions. Transcendent is cut off from structural, structural from personal, personal from interior. The wounds multiply, and through them drains away the blood that is the power of preaching and, ultimately, of Christian living.

We will take a closer look at this by focusing on two dimensions, the personal and the structural, which are often dealt with at each other's expense. Hunger is in focus this Sunday morning in Little Church of Denomination One in Nicetown. The preacher has decided that the issue must be dealt with at a personal level (with perhaps a touch of the interior thrown in). Many people in the congregation know about the Shackles, who sometimes attend church, but only irregularly, and then exuding discomfort. The preacher is concerned enough about confidentiality that he does not mention the Shackles by name, but he offers up here and there a clue to titillate the curious ear. Like the Shackles, his unnamed case study is of a poor family eking out a living on welfare. The family lives in a shack at the top of the hill, on the edge of sparse woods, the trees only partially obscuring the landfill on the other side.

Our preacher then paints a moving picture of what life is like for this family, with the children going to bed hungry and the parents going to bed hungry and angry: Angry at themselves because they can't provide a better life for their children. Angry at whatever nameless entity out there is to be blamed for unemployment lines. Angry even (in that way anger has of spreading into areas where you wish it wouldn't) at their children for being constant reminders of their own failure. Then the preacher portrays a family made happier by food bags and donations of fresh-baked pies. He does a powerful job; by the end of the sermon he has convinced many that something has to be done to help those Shackles.

There are plenty of hazards to be negotiated in the course of offering that help, including the likelihood that any aid offered to the Shackles is apt to be tinged with a paternalism and a brisk do-goodism that can provoke as much resentment as gratitude. Still, some genuine and needed balm may flow the Shackles' way, and it is the rare sermon that catalyzes that much concrete reaction, so some praise is due it.

If the sermon has emerged from a well-rounded preaching diet, one that wrestles with the full complexity of the gospel's application in a complex world, it may be what is needed at this time in this context. If this kind of sermon is always what our preacher preaches, then it is flawed. It gives its hearers tools for dealing with one specific need in narrowly defined ways but gives them no significant insight into the broader dynamics whose winds rage not only against one family on a hill but against millions of families on other hills—and in valleys and on plains.

On the other side of town, hunger is also the focus in Big

Church of Denomination Two. But our preacher here has not been long out of seminary and she knows the weaknesses of preaching saturated in the personal or interior dimensions. She knows that when cars keep sliding off the curve and down the hill the *ultimate* solution is building a better barricade rather than binding up those bleeding on the rocks below. So she preaches not about the Shackles but about the social structures that shackle human beings. She talks about great economic forces and intricate government policies and dissects the ways they conspire to cause people to go hungry.

She preaches well; when she is done the people are angry, angry at unjust economic structures and government policies that favor the rich. Some are ready to form a group dedicated to influencing a corporation deemed particularly exploitative; others are ready to go out and plead fiercely with the President and Congress to stop balancing the budget on the backs of the hungry.

There are hazards to be negotiated here, as well. The situation may indeed be akin to that dangerous road—and efforts to resolve the problem of hunger at a structural level may prove no more effective than would the person with no understanding of car handling and road engineering who tried to analyze and solve the problem of the dangerous curve. Or it may be that problem and solution are correctly understood but the structures in need of change are too entrenched and cumbersome to respond. David is facing Goliath, but no pebble and no vulnerable spot to hit can be found.

Despite such hazards, to the extent that our preacher has managed to stimulate concern for structural change, she is to be applauded. She has helped her hearers grasp the broader picture, and they are likely to do more than carry a fish up the hill to the Shackles. "Carry a fish to a family and feed the family for a day, but teach a family to fish and feed the family for a lifetime!" they may exclaim. And how right they will be.

This sermon as well, however, may be flawed. All is well if it, too, is one in a well-rounded mix of sermons. But if this is the only kind of sermon Big Church is hearing, it focuses too narrowly on the structural. The Shackles may be partially victims of structural oppression, but the Shackles are also still up there going to bed hungry even as Big Church turns structural change into a project. It is also likely that either the church is attended by a disproportionate number of people skilled in understanding the abstractions involved in dealing with structural issues, or those excited by the sermon are a nonrepresentative minority.

The preachers at Little and Big churches have risked weakening their sermons by grappling only one-dimensionally with a multidimensional issue. This is the case not only in terms of the dimensions we have been discussing but also in relation to levels of abstraction and concretion identified by Lowry: we tend to experience the personal (or interior) aspects of life in more *concrete* ways and the larger political, economic, or social structures that impinge on our personal lives in more *abstract* ways. The personal dimension can certainly be dealt with abstractly—as in abstruse psychological or relational theories. And the structural dimension can be dealt with concretely—as in a newspaper report on the concrete implications of an act of Congress.

The tendency remains, however, for preaching that deals with the personal to be concrete and intimate and for preaching that deals with the structural to be abstract and distant. So another way of talking about what the First and Big Church preachers have done is to see each as grappling with only one side of what Lowry calls "the problem of abstract-concrete polarity."[2]

Integrating the Dimensions Through Story

How might the gash separating concrete and abstract, personal and structural, be healed? How might one hold together both the Shackles and the forces shackling them? One approach is to use the "abstraction ladder," to go up and down the ladder from abstract-structural-general to concrete-personal-specific or vice versa, aiming to "present the particularity of eggs *and* also provide baskets to put them in."[3]

This method, though helpful, is limited because it helps integrate a sermon's *content* but does not provide a *form* through which that integration can naturally flow. That form is, of course, story. Says Lowry:

Note how in a story . . . the polarities of abstract/ concrete and general/specific are overcome. The story moves through inner and outer action, development of character, and progression of plot—and by so doing, the extremes of abstract and concrete are merged into event. In a specific moment of action the listeners make their own paradigmatic abstractions, and conversely a general concept is presented before our very ears in event. And the form story takes transcends such polarities with power because that's the way we actually live our own lives.[4]

Story is the needle knitting all the polarities and dichotomies we have been discussing into one seamless fabric. Preaching that does not possess some such means as story for rubbing ointment into the gashes between the levels of our existence is preaching operating at half power. This is all the more true because the dimensions are hazier in real life than in theory: the transcendent weaves its way through the structural and the personal and the interior; the personal feeds the structural and the structural shapes the personal—or is it the other way around? We experience the transcendent by focusing on the immanent—or do we not see all the wonder in the immanent because we exclude the transcendent?

We could continue, and that might be helpful; it might also short-circuit our attempts to comprehend. It is precisely that overloading of minds which the preacher risks when trying to deal holistically with complicated matters. Yet life is like that, a tangle of multidimensional dynamics that must be dealt with in their totality if preaching is to grapple meaningfully with the real issues of the real world. That is why preaching which wants to take that totality seriously needs story. We will leave to the experts the more technical reasons for story's power to knit together polarities without losing itself in confusion, but among the more obvious reasons is the presence in a good story of some sort of *movement*. Movement in story is like the skeleton in a body. All kinds of things get stuck together to form a body, but the skeleton gives them all shape and substance and recognizable, graspable form. All kinds of things can be grafted together in a story, but that thread of movement, of development, of unfolding process gives the mind something it can hold on to, something upon which to hang all the complexity and give it manageable form.

Leo Tolstoy demonstrated this in his great novel *War and Peace,* which in one translation goes on for 1,399 pages.[5] It follows innumerable characters through countless developments. The face-to-face interaction of characters at the personal level and their interior thoughts and feelings are described in detail. At the same time, this more concrete dimension is described within the framework of the abstract and structural background—the battles and forces of the Napoleonic conflict with Russia of the early 1800s—against which it unfolds. Underlying it all is Tolstoy's belief that, while humans can make some choices within the context of their presence in the broad sweep of history, history's forces sweep them forward in ways beyond their individual control.

What Tolstoy presents in *War and Peace* is an awesome tangle of events and motivations and people and structures and philosophical assumptions—yet this is not a textbook but a *story,* and so the tangle is manageable. The thread of movement allows for the almost unconscious assimilation of data that would leave one bewildered if presented in purely propositional form. And the assimilation takes place in an integrated way; the many dimensions are intertwined and intermingled just as they are in real life.

As intricate as is the tangle Tolstoy presents, the tangle with which the Christian preacher must cope is more intricate yet. The preacher is dealing ultimately with all reality, both seen and unseen, with reality in all its entanglements and mysteries, heights and depths. How much more even than Tolstoy, given this mandate, does the preacher need story as a vehicle for mediating the gospel in a way that is true to life's complexities, yet accessible to persons with limited capacity to grasp such tangles!

The Dimensions of the Christian Story

If the preacher is to deal with the gospel as story, he or she will have to come to some conclusions about what Story is being told. The way the Story is told varies in broad ways from denomination to denomination and across the spectrum of theological perspectives; each smaller grouping, each congregation or family or individual, will also appropriate and tell the Story in ways that uniquely take into account their specific contexts. The preacher who tells the Story must thus make some decisions about how to tell it in her or his setting.

In what follows we will share *our* version, the Story that has emerged from our particular settings. We know there are other ways to tell the Story; we share our version not to impose it on others but to provide a guide to the kind of work any preacher will need to do before using the Story as the skeleton upon which to build sermons about social issues. We will deal only with one part of the Story, albeit a central one, and will not try to encompass the whole, a task better left to systematic theologians with a narrative bent.

What we want to do, then, is to show ways in which preaching that respects the story element of the gospel can weave together the structural, personal, interior, and transcendent dimensions—and their countless permutations. We particularly want to examine what happens when that part of the gospel which deals with evil—particularly as it is manifested through fallen principalities and powers—and Christ's atoning work is treated as a multidimensional story. We start from the assumption that, though God intended creation to be good, it is now beset by evil. Creation is fallen. To talk about the fall, or the evil that consequently slithers through the world and our lives in it, is to deal with matters that can quickly become technical. So our first task, as we undertake telling of evil and its vanquishing, is to narrow the scope of our project.

Remembering the focus of this book helps us: Though *all* dimensions of social issues must be taken into account as one approaches the preaching task, in this book we are giving priority to the structural dimension. We are concerned with the broad—often global—sweep of many issues. We do, certainly, want to link the structural with the more personal, intimate, or transcendent, but such dimensions are not our first concern. How they relate to the structural dimension is the question we want to address. Thus in telling the Story of evil and of Christ victorious we *do* want to grapple with evil, whose presence creates the suffering, pain, and brokenness without which there would be no great need to preach about justice, peace, liberation. And we do want to touch on ways Christ's atonement manifests itself in all dimensions. But our focus on the structural will control and limit how we do so.

The Structural Dimension

Structural evil then becomes an appropriate starting point. That leads to an examination of biblical material that many scholars believe pertinent to such a discussion—material that comments on the "principalities and powers." There is in the New Testament, particularly in its Pauline portions, a body of references to a mysterious but real dimension of evil. Sometimes the reference is to "thrones and dominions," sometimes to "elemental spirits," sometimes to "angels and archangels," sometimes to "law" or "knowledge," sometimes to "principalities and powers."[6] As G. B. Caird notes, the concepts that underlie such references are "built into the very fabric of Paul's thought" and are mentioned in every epistle except Philemon.[7]

Though the nuances of each reference could be investigated, John Howard Yoder makes a case for treating them in a unified way: "Probably for Paul each term had its own very precise and technical meaning; [thus] they are not simply synonyms standing parallel. Still, the best we can do today is to come to some understanding about the general trend of meaning which the total body of thought has for us."[8]

Following Yoder, we will speak of the fallen "principalities and powers" as a general way of referring to the powers of evil. The life and death and resurrection of Christ, viewed from within this understanding, is then seen in the perspective of engaging with and defeating the powers, robbing them of their potential for evil. Within this context, the *Christus Victor* view of the atonement popularized by Gustaf Aulén becomes an important way of conceiving Christ's mission, whose work fulfills the central drama of the Bible, which is "the war that God fights . . . against the hostile powers, against all the evil that holds mankind in bondage." The atonement, Aulén asserts, "must be fitted into this drama. The Atonement is the turning point of the war that God fights with the powers of evil."[9]

But even if one narrows all the references to the powers or related terms down to one general statement, and if one then applies to that general perspective the notion that Christ has overcome the powers, what exactly *are* the powers? At what level, exactly, does Christ defeat them? One influential strand of interpretation suggests that the powers are *structures,* and that what Christ primarily overcomes is structural evil. This approach owes much to Hendrikus Berkhof, who argues that, for Paul,

> life is ruled by a series of Powers. He speaks of time (present and future), of space (depth and height), of life and death, of politics and philosophy, of public opinion and Jewish law, of pious tradition and the fateful course of the stars. Apart from Christ man is at the mercy of these Powers. They encompass, carry, and guide his life. The demands of the present, fear for the future, state and society, life and death, tradition and morality—they are all our "guardians and trustees," the forces which hold together the world and the life of men and preserve them from chaos.[10]

Yoder, summarizing this, identifies four broad structures—religious, moral, political, and intellectual—which in our day serve as analogues to what Paul in his day called the powers. Yoder argues that there is some sense in which these structures are always more powerful than the "mere sum total of the individuals composing them."[11] The ancients, like Paul, were trying to grasp this tendency of structures to take on a life of their own, a life somehow larger than life, when they used such symbols of the supernatural as angels to describe them.

Our modern, secular perspective, with its view that angels are remnants of an outdated worldview, need not (according to this approach) think of the powers as possessing some sort of angelic quality. But such symbols, properly translated and demythologized, still carry meaning today, helping us view the powers as a skein of interactions lying outside anyone's full comprehension or control.

If the powers are viewed as structures, it is important to note that they are not automatically evil. Yoder reminds us that "they were part of the good creation of God. Society and history, even nature, would be impossible without regularity, system, order—and this need God provided for. The universe . . . was made in an ordered form and 'it was good.' "[12] A structure is not, merely by virtue of being a structure, evil. This suggests that to overcome the evil of the structures is not to dissolve them and plunge the world into anarchy; it is not in the absence of institutions and systems and governments that utopia arrives.

We do, however, often experience the structural powers as evil, as demonic powers, because they *are* fallen. They preserve the world from anarchy, so vestiges of their original goodness remain and are not to be minimized. But, because fallen, they also imprison the world. The systems of government that divide the world into manageable entities keep it hovering on the brink of nuclear annihilation. Economic systems that have brought wealth to many have also impoverished and exploited many others. Jim Wallis, seeing this good-but-fallen nature of those structures manifested in society's institutions, says that "institutions, rather than functioning to serve and edify human life in the world, have become distorted, usurping, dominating, and even demonic in character and function."[13]

As can be seen, those who view the Story through the prism of powers-as-structures theology believe a primary way evil manifests itself in the world is through those structural powers which rebel against their divine mandate to preserve a just and peaceful order and ask to be served in their own right, to become idols, false gods. In this view, civil religion, with its religious reverence for such a symbol of the nation as the flag, tends to support the transformation of the governmental power into false god. Overcoming this evil means calling the government to renounce its role as false god and return to the more modest role of standing as dike against chaos.

The evil to be overcome is thus the evil that manifests itself in the tangible, immanent structures of this world. Our model for the overcoming is provided by Christ, who courageously faced down the powers even to death; who through resurrection unmasked the powers, demonstrating that they are not the controllers of life, the gods of the world, but only servants of the one true God. Nations think they give and take life. Jesus tells them and shows them that in the end that is God's job.

Such an understanding can enrich the theology of any preacher struggling to connect Christianity with the social issues of the day. It suggests that the social/political/economic realm is not marginal but crucial to the outworking of Christian faith. It provides handholds the preacher can grasp in climbing toward an understanding of social issues and the ability to preach about them.

There are weaknesses here, however. Those who espouse this approach seem sometimes reluctant to integrate it with other dimensions of the struggle against evil. Yoder, for one, seems to shy away from the nonstructural dimensions of the Story. He does not want Christ's atonement, which he views primarily as a grappling with the structural powers, to be applied too quickly to personal issues: "The cross of Calvary was not a difficult family situation, not a frustration of visions of personal fulfillment, a crushing debt or a nagging in-law; it was the political, legally to be expected result of a moral clash with the powers ruling his society."[14] Neither does he want to see "cross" language applied to the interior dimensions, to "subjective brokenness, the renunciation of pride and self-will."[15]

Yoder is also suspicious of views that take into account the transcendent implications of the cross:

> The Powers have been defeated not by some sort of cosmic hocus-pocus but by the concreteness of the cross; the impact of the cross upon them is not the working of magical words nor the fulfillment of a legal contract calling for the shedding of innocent blood, but the sovereign presence, within the structures of creaturely orderliness, of Jesus the kingly claimant and of the church who is herself a structure and a power in society.[16]

Yoder understandably wants to highlight the structural implications of the gospel and may be partly reacting against versions of Christianity that have failed to take into account the crucial structural dimension; any of us who have done this need to be taken to task for it. Since this may be one of Yoder's aims, his stance is not to be quickly faulted. At the same time, for those who stress the structural there is the risk of falling prey to the dichotomizing weakness. Evil exists at levels other than the structural. The

Christ who unmasks the pretensions of social or national powers also inveighs against the lusts of the heart, casts demons out of a Gerasene man, stills storms.

It seems a flattening of perspective to ignore the possibility that the Christ Story, though including the structural dimension, has heights and depths that the thoroughly structural perspective misses. What is one to say to those who, though enslaved by structural powers, though tortured or jailed or hungry, have been transformed by a power that sets them free within even though they are still bound without (the interior dimension)? Or to those who, like the Shackles, are aided by relief efforts even though structural causes of their pain remain in place (the personal dimension)? Or to those who testify—though the alcohol or drug cultures still remain in place—that they have been mysteriously and miraculously freed of their addictions, that the bonds of sin have been broken (the transcendent dimension)? Have they not also been liberated by their risen Lord? Should not the preacher address those dimensions of the issues as well?

The Personal Dimension

While it is important for preaching about social issues to grapple with those aggregates of people and forces that we have been calling structural powers, the preacher cannot ignore the individual parts which together form them if listeners are to be offered hope that they can affect the larger structures. Though all of us live each day within an intricate webbing of structures, we experience them not only in their impersonal guise but also in more personal ways.

The struggle against evil takes on personal form and includes faces and shapes and names; it unfolds in a dimension in which the hungry are not just faceless victims of global forces but Shackles living on a hill. Nuclear war may explode not just because hopelessly complex international forces conspired to send the mushroom clouds soaring but also because individual workers built a warhead, and because rich consumers loved a luxurious life-style so much that when Jesus told them to sell what they had they turned away sadly. They preferred to defend their life-style to the death with missiles rather than give it up to save their souls and the world. They were, of course, tangled up in forces none of them, individually, could control; they also made personal decisions that fueled instead of countered those larger forces.

Preaching that proclaims Jesus' defeat of evil at this level will help hearers transcend the numbness, the sense of futility, that comes from finding ourselves at the mercy of forces too large to influence. As preaching exposes its hearers to this nitty-gritty, daily-grind level of the issues, and as it encourages change at this level, it offers hope that such change can happen. It supports change when it does occur—it constructs a boat in which a voyage on the ocean of suppressed feeling we discussed in chapter 1 can be undertaken.

Such preaching helps hearers understand that they participate in and are empowered by Jesus' victory when they wrestle with the role their jobs play in the larger structures, when they spend Saturday morning in a soup kitchen, when they sing a child tenderly to sleep and through that tenderness wordlessly share with the child the wild news that Jesus has overcome the world.

The Interior Dimension

But the Story of the vanquishing of evil unfolds in a yet more intimate dimension. Within people things go on that have a bearing on the broader dimensions. People experience life not only as members of great structures or as participants in personal interactions. They experience it also as great battles and triumphs and defeats within. To that level, too, the preacher must speak. As is true of all dimensions, there are many ways to interpret what goes on within. John Sanford, who has attempted to integrate Christianity and the thought of Carl Jung, offers one approach. He argues, for example, that each of us possesses a shadow, the "adversary within ourself . . . who contradicts the outer front . . . the Mr. Hyde to our Dr. Jekyll."[17]

The more we try to suppress this dark side of ourselves and pretend there is no stirring of anger, jealousy, or perverted longing within us, the more powerful it becomes. It is the shadow, oozing out around the edges of the seemingly sweet person, that sometimes gives us a whiff of buried evil. By suppressing our shadow, by forcing it down into our unconscious depths, we give evil a chance to take control of our lives; unaware of its influence, we are unable to counter its power. The part, like cancerous cells, takes over the whole.[18]

How are we to summon the valor to face honestly the shadows within? Through Jesus Christ, suggests Don S. Browning. He notes that "brokenness involves a rigid and idolatrous dependence on some values and feelings at the cost of estrangement from others." Then he argues that Christ, through the atonement, accepted "repressed and denied creation in sinful man."[19] Jesus died to heal the brokenness caused by our rebellion against God. Jesus died, to put it quite simply, for our sins, and cleansed them, making it clear that God's words to us are the words Jesus uttered to the woman caught in adultery: "Neither do I condemn you." With those healing words stirring in our depths we can face our dark sides—and be transformed by a paradox: when we face our darkness, and accept that it is indeed within us and often possesses us, its power for evil can be overcome.

Preaching sensitive to this dimension will help its hearers understand that when the darkness within is not faced, those possessed by their unadmitted shadows may view themselves as righteousness incarnate and their opponents as the embodiment of evil. They may then, invoking God on their side, righteously prepare the weapons to kill those devils. Having faced their shadows, on the other hand, they can admit there is some evil within themselves and just possibly some good within the enemy. No longer need they be convinced that an unambiguous battle between good and evil is what the superpowers are waging. They will thus be more ready to work toward some sort of coexistence. The issue is a global one—yet battle in the solitary human soul is relevant to it.

The Transcendent Dimension

One dimension, the transcendent, remains. The dimensions of the Story would not be fully explored without a voyage into mystery. But precisely because mystery is what we are trying to fathom, we will use the form that we have stressed is most open to the mysterious and transcendent—story. In this case, it is story as told by Charles Williams. Dillistone says:

> Perhaps the most ambitious recent attempts to reinterpret the work of Christ in terms of a . . . victory over the powers of evil are to be found in the imaginative novels of Charles Williams and C. S. Lewis. Each of these writers had a profound sense of the reality of evil. The universe for them was not simply defective in certain respects, imperfect because unfulfilled; rather it was groaning and travailing, the scene of a grim conflict, the field of a real battle in which more than human forces were engaged.[20]

For Charles Williams, the universe was a place where the transcendent and the immanent, the temporal and the eternal, the ordinary and the mysterious, met and merged. To read a Williams novel is to be taking a prosaic voyage in a car or having a perfectly ordinary conversation with a friend only to be suddenly confronted with one's double, or a sorcerer, or a snowstorm swirling through earth and heaven and hell wrapped into one. In Williams's world an event taking place in one time can have a direct impact on some other time, or a sick person can be healed when another, through love, takes over the illness. To encounter Williams is to wonder if indeed the demonic or angelic elements of the Christ Story can be that easily translated into modern, demythologized terms.

Williams's vision and its resistance to demythologization gives particular power (or absurdity, if one finds his novels uncompelling) to his portrayal of evil. This is evident in *Descent Into Hell*, in which Williams tells a number of stories as he examines evil. One of them is about Wentworth, a distinguished historian. Wentworth wants to be loved by Adela Hunt, a young woman attracted to him and his distinguished status. But to love and be loved by her, he will have to enter the world of normal human relations, the world in which loving means hard, bruising work. This, being too self-absorbed, too infatuated with the dream of effortless love, he cannot do.

Then the mysterious erupts in the guise of a succubus—a

demonic entity in the form of Adela. By the power of his infatuation Wentworth has created her, this shadow of the real woman he is too lazy to love. Wentworth senses what she really is, but he is too far gone in his self-absorption to care, so he continues down a path of choices favoring evil, favoring cotton-candy illusion over hard—though ultimately fulfilling—reality. Finally he descends into hell itself, the natural outcome of the journey he has made of his life.

It is not entirely clear just where Wentworth is at this point—whether in some sort of psychological torment, or a more literal place. But that is the point—mystery. Exactly what evil may do to us, precisely what may be the parameters of the hell to which it brings us, Williams doesn't say. What he does want to say is that evil and hell cannot be easily flattened into our modern understandings. Evil—and good—have power that can transcend easy and logical and secular analyses.

There is another story in the book, one with a different ending. It is the story of an unskilled assistant who is hired by a construction company during a time of high unemployment. He has been out of work for a long time, and he is "hungry . . . ill . . . clumsy and slow." Though his intentions are good, he doesn't perform to company standards and is fired. Broken, he commits suicide and, in much of the rest of the book, wanders through the world of the dead.

Another character, Margaret Anstruther, lives a life of love, which in Williams's view can penetrate even into the land of death. So the dead man moans in his misery, aching, unlike Wentworth, to live a life transcending self-absorption. He moans, but as he moans, Margaret intercedes for him—prays, in effect, for him—and the moan becomes more than his: "As if the sound released something greater than itself, another moan answered it. . . . The groan was at once [one of] dereliction of power and creation of power. In it, far off, beyond vision in the depths of all the worlds, a god, unamenable to death, awhile endured and died." And in the dead man, "also something suffered and was free."[21]

Preaching that senses the power of this dimension, mysterious though it is, and difficult though it is to grasp in propositional form, will be preaching imbued with an aura of awe and high drama. It will convey to its hearers the conviction that to enter the Story is to descend to the depths of reality and into the land of death itself, and wrestle with the power of evil. It will convey that struggle. And then it will echo the moan of the god who awhile endures then dies; who moans the moans of all the world; who takes the moans into the land of the dead in order to return with exaltation—with moans turned into shouts of joy—to the land of the living.

The Dimensions Knitted Together

This, then, is the story we have been telling: once upon a time—after sadness had come to the world, and the people were broken by good powers turned evil, as they wrestled with the evil in their personal lives and in their depths, as they dimly sensed that more was at stake than could be easily grasped—someone came to lace the sadness with new joy. He came to challenge the evil of the powers and in some measure to give back to them their original good function as dikes holding back chaos. He came to release people from the personal sins and inner lusts that helped fuel the evil of the powers. He came to endure awhile, then die and rise again.

He challenged evil, and it resisted; murderously, it resisted, breaking the man on the cross that stood on Golgotha as a symbol of evil's power. For some few days it symbolized evil's power, and then the meaning of the symbol was reversed and evil itself hung on the cross, which from that time on would stand as a symbol of the defeat of evil and Jesus' victory.

This story, as we have suggested, unfolded with a complexity rivaling and surpassing that of the story Tolstoy tells in *War and Peace.* It unfolded then and still does today with the kind of complexity Garrison Keillor unfolds from another angle. Keillor, host of American Public Radio's "A Prairie Home Companion" and spinner of tales about a small, semifictional Minnesota town called Lake Wobegon, told once about a friend's temptation toward adultery.

The friend had just been demoted at the college where he worked. At home he felt that he was an underappreciated drudge. Then along came the proverbial work associate who properly appreciated his unsung abilities. He decided, from that vantage point, that adultery looked pretty nice, and he scheduled with his associate a business trip during which he could enjoy it.

The day came; he kissed his wife and went out the door to sit on his front lawn and wait for his associate to pick him up. While he sat, looking forward to adultery, he looked up and down the street, at the houses of friends and neighbors, and thought about the good things those houses stood for. He thought about the little routine things going on in each, the countless interconnected little acts that combine to make life decent and good. There, while in the other houses people ate and washed dishes and changed diapers and thus affirmed their commitment to each other, he waited for his adultery.

He began to look forward less to it. He began to wonder what would happen once he began to strain the fragile tissue binding him and the people in his community together. He said, "I saw that we all depend on each other; I saw that although I thought my sins could be secret, that they would be no more secret than an earthquake. All these houses and all these families—my infidelity will somehow shake them."

He imagined the drinking water becoming polluted, and "noxious gases [coming] out of the ventilators in the elementary school." He imagined a little girl down the way trying to cross the street, and of his adultery somehow tearing at the fabric of what should have been and allowing the little girl to be injured. He imagined his minister thinking, "What the hell! I'm not going to give that sermon on the poor!"[22]

Keillor is trying to say something akin to what we have been trying to say: We *are* all living out a Story threading its way through a tangle of structures, personal interactions, internal dynamics, and mysterious forces that must be taken into account if the Story is to be understood. Yet the complexity need not throw us into despair. It need not do so precisely because what we are dealing with *is* a story, and only the teller of the Story, rather than any one character in it, is responsible for grasping its totality. Our responsibility as characters is not to master the Story, but to sense the ways our particular role is linked to its multidimensional texture.

Our responsibility as preachers, then, is to help our listeners see themselves not merely as isolated individuals struggling in piecemeal and therefore usually ineffective ways with their own woes and the woes of those broken by principalities and powers run amok. They are, instead, characters and potential heroes in a cosmic drama, a drama in which each part interacts with every other part, so that not only working to change structures that cause hunger but also deciding to resist adultery can, in powerful and mysterious ways, move the drama forward. It is therefore not only the obvious heroes—the Martin Luther King, Jr.'s and the Oscar Romeros—who wrestle with the large issues, but even the demoted college professor sitting on a lawn refusing finally to put a bandage on his broken parts by breaking other lives.

The Christian Story and the Church

We have now explored most of what we intended in this chapter. But in the manner of good storytellers, we have saved until last a climactic hope—the hope that the cosmic script will be acted out not just by individuals but by a community of people. It is in the church, if anywhere, that what we have been talking about can actually be lived out.

This is not to deny that it is possible for the Story to help shape even societies that do not believe in it or feel any particular burden to live it out. A government can be viewed as a principality and power that was created to serve a good purpose but that tends to degenerate into demonic self-aggrandizement. The Christian with such an understanding will have a vision of what a good government might look like—one that carries out the good function of holding back chaos without expecting its citizens to worship it as a god. Guided by such a vision, the Christian (at least in a democratic society) can use the prerogatives of citizenship, including the vote—or, when voting is not enough, such methods as boycotts and demonstrations—to call the government to live out the vision without demanding that the government accept the Christian *source* of the vision. In the United States, this would often mean allowing a Christian vision to open eyes to the guarantees already set forth in the

Constitution—guarantees that the government can be called upon to protect without invoking religion.

We have been assuming, as we have progressed through this chapter, that this calling of the powers to their rightful role is part of the goal of preaching about social issues; but we do not believe that it is primarily in this more secular arena that the Story has its first and most immediate impact. In the end, yes, all powers will be transformed and function under Christ's reign to spread shalom across the new heaven and new earth.

But during this phase of the Story, it is in the church that the defeat of the powers' evil will be most evident—or should be, for the church is all too weak in carrying out its role in the Story. The church is that gathering of people who have decided to risk their lives for the hope that God really is telling a Story. To the extent that the church lives out this faith, it becomes the place in which the outlines of the Story are most clearly seen. If part of the Story is the message that evil—at all levels—has been ultimately overcome by Jesus, then the church will give concrete shape to that reality. It will become, as Jim Wallis puts it, an "alternative social reality, a living testimony to the kingdom of God in the world." Wallis, whose comments focus on the structural dimension but can be extrapolated to others, calls the church to be a new community witnessing

> to the fact that Christ has triumphed over the principalities and powers of the world system (Col. 2:15). The rebellious powers have been disarmed by Christ and their final defeat is sure. The structures of class, race, sex, ideology, government, money and power need not determine us any longer. The victory of Christ liberates people from their slavery. Their ultimate authority has been broken. The Christian community is called to show the reality of the victory of Christ over the powers of the world.[23]

One of us attended a denominational conference organized to wrestle with this very issue. How was this particular denomination to make concrete its claim to offer the world a foretaste of the kingdom of shalom toward which the Story is heading? As will likely ever be the case with such conferences, nothing happened to guarantee a dramatic new in-breaking of the kingdom. But there were swirls of hope, moments when the spine chilled as, for an instant here and there, the grandeur of that toward which we feebly grope broke through. Farmers, businesspeople, professionals, rural people, urban folk—all were there, each with concerns and ideas shaped by their respective contexts.

As the weekend wore on, it became clearer and clearer that even though participants had come from across the country and usually didn't know each other, all were caught up in an interlocking web. A Minnesota farming couple passionately shared the pain of the many lean years, years of walking through beloved fields that any week or month might host the crowds hungry for a bargain at a farm foreclosure auction. A speaker noted that the same pain that had devastated that couple had yielded profits to businesspeople in the denomination, whose supermarket prices could in turn drop to reflect declining farm produce prices—yielding bargains to help a poor mother feed her hungry children more easily.

All were in the same church community—yet the loss of one could be the gain of another. Those at the conference wrestled with the hard reality that the forces of evil, which in so many dimensions oppress and exploit and crush, were not just wreaking their havoc out there but were slithering right through the church community. What might it take, some wondered, to challenge that evil in concrete ways by transforming the church into an "alternate social reality"? How might that particular denomination challenge the marketer of farm produce enjoying rich times to help the farmer through the lean times, and vice versa (if vice versa for the smaller farmers ever comes)? How might persons in lucrative professions help those planning to enter low-wage professions like social work get their training without ending up broken by debt?

The dreaming went on. Much of it will not soon be more than a dream, yet the dream was carried home to local congregations, to those entities often more malleable than denominations. Even there only a few of the dreams will survive the moment of waking. Yet some will. Sometimes the well will make meals for the sick. Sometimes the wealthy will support a loan fund from which the poorer can draw low-interest loans. Sometimes men and women will submit mutually to each other rather than fight for power, and black and white will learn to value each other. Sometimes those gifted in communing with the transcendent, the mysterious—with God—will pray, and who knows what eucatastrophic things may happen then!

3

The Biblical Story's
Perspective on Key Issues

In chapter 1 we saw that preaching about the large social issues needs to be open to the transcendent—open to the good news of God's irruption into history and into our lives within the stream of history, to Tolkien's eucatastrophe, and to his "joy beyond the walls of the world, poignant as grief." In chapter 2 we wrestled with the need for such preaching to take into account the multidimensional nature of the issues. And in both chapters we emphasized the importance of story as a form open to the transcendent and able to weave the dimensions of our lives and the issues into a coherent whole.

What we have not dealt with yet is the role played by perspective in shaping how we deal with these facets of preaching about social issues. Much of what we have said could be applied in vastly different ways. We have made much, for example, of the need for preaching to throb with eucatastrophic hope. But from what perspective do we evaluate what is good and what is bad catastrophe?

White South Africa and apartheid are beleaguered at the time of this writing. If in some unexpected way black hopes were thwarted and apartheid was strengthened, would that be a eucatastrophe, a glorious event to be thundered from white pulpits across the land? We think not, yet perhaps some *would* think so. Why? What ingredient is missing from their perspective, allowing its distortion? What ingredient do our perspectives need if they are to suffer minimal distortion?

The Principle of Reversal

If in fact they and we are living out stories, then it may be helpful to investigate ingredients of story we have not yet emphasized. Frederick Buechner offers clues as he looks at one of the marks of fairy stories, which is that things in them often turn out not to be what they seem:

> The beautiful queen is really a witch in disguise, and to open the lid of the golden casket is to be doomed. Not only does evil come disguised in the world of the fairy tale but often good does too. Who could guess that the little gray man asking for bread is a great magician who holds in his hands the power of life and death? One thinks . . . of *King Lear*. . . . In the world of *King Lear* it is the wicked ones like Goneril and Regan who go about in gorgeous robes, and the good ones, the compassionate and innocent ones, who wander disguised in a fool's motley or the rags of beggars and madmen.[1]

Things are not what they seem. The unexpected erupts. Or, as Lowry puts it, "a strange corner is turned. The thing that could not possibly happen, does, and the obvious eventuality does not."[2] Lowry calls this the *principle of reversal* and explores ways it crops up in "literature, humor, television stories and puzzles."[3] And also in our life stories: "The bungling researcher whose proven incompetence has thwarted everyone else's work for so long that now we come to expect it, arrives at the office of the departmental head for dismissal and stumbles onto the solution while tripping through the office doorway."[4]

This principle of reversal obviously does not offer a fail-safe way of avoiding errors in perspective. It is not a clear-cut rule to be applied in a precise way in the expectation of precise results. It functions more as a warning and as a hope to be explored throughout life—a warning that what seems to us good, right, and to be expected may not be; a hope that what seems tragic, hopeless, and to be expected also may not be. In this chapter we want to explore that warning and that hope and their relation to preaching about social issues.

As we explore, we will not claim to offer cut-and-dried ways of safeguarding correct perspective. We know perspective is a tricky thing shaped in countless subtle ways, so subtle that the perspective we are using to struggle toward a correct perspective may itself be warped. We will nevertheless risk highlighting ways in which recognition of the element of reversal in both story in general and the biblical story in particular might help shape appropriate perspective. We will then relate this, and other ingredients of good social-issue preaching we have identified in preceding chapters, to specific and key issues.

Reversal as an Ingredient of Story

Turning first to more extended illustration of the way reversal functions in story, we want to take a look at the movie *One Flew Over the Cuckoo's Nest.* (We might note that we want to be held accountable only for what we explicitly affirm about the movie, not for the movie in its totality, flawed as it is by a sometimes simplistic and stereotypic treatment of its topic.) The film tells the story of what happens when Randall P. McMurphy is committed to a mental hospital whose inmates are under the totalitarian rule of Nurse Ratchett. McMurphy is an ambiguous figure; it is never clear to what extent he is healthier than his commitment might indicate, and to what extent he is, in fact, a psychopathic character whose pathology nevertheless possesses potential to work good.

What happens when McMurphy enters the scene is less ambiguous, however. He immediately shakes things up. How one is to view the shake-up is the point at which the question of perspective enters the picture. Nurse Ratchett holds the power. She is happy with her role in the story. From her perspective McMurphy and the changes he threatens are a bad thing indeed. On the other hand, the inmates, the powerless ones, have little to lose and much potentially to gain from change. They stand ready to embrace such a change agent as McMurphy.

Change the system McMurphy does, rumbling defiantly and maniacally and insouciantly through that gray place. When eucatastrophe comes, when a good catastrophe bursts the walls of her institution, Nurse Ratchett does not understand. She thought the good news would come on her terms; it comes, instead, in a reversal of her terms, and she, with no eyes to see or ears to hear its glory, sees instead only evil to be overcome. What happens to her is what happens to all of us who reflect upon our stories and particularly the biblical story without comprehending the ingredient of reversal.

McMurphy's rumbles of defiance deepen into thunder, and he leads his fellow inmates in a breakout from the hospital. There they go, those whose faces were once dead, testifying only to the reality of Thorazine coursing through veins and decades of stultifying institutionalization calcifying bones. There they go, those so often thought incapable by society (and the Nurse Ratchetts it puts in place to ratify and carry out its opinions) of anything but empty stares and puffing endless cigarettes, and rocking and jerking and twitching rhythmically but aimlessly on, forever. There they go, with McMurphy who has commandeered a school bus. On that bus they travel to the ocean. At the edge of the sea they find a boat, and in that boat they go fishing. There they go, only now not with faces dead and bodies twitching, but with faces and bodies shimmering and shaking with delight as the boat surges out to the deep blue sea.

For them, good catastrophe has befallen; the mighty reversal has occurred. The psychopath has proved savior and the mad have proved capable of a joy the sane in the story can only fear. But for Nurse Ratchett this is plain old bad catastrophe, to be undone as soon as possible. Will we preachers avoid making the same mistake? Will we avoid turning our sermons into police boats screeching out to pull in the escaped inmates, when in fact with our sermons we should be making the fishing boats in which all the world's inmates can head out into the sun and the waves and the wind of salvation? Those are the questions that need to burn in us as we ponder this matter of reversal and what can happen to us if we are blind to it.

Reversal and the Biblical Story

Especially ought those questions to burn when we turn to the biblical story, in which the ingredient of reversal is doubled and tripled. To turn a page in that book of stories and Story which is the Bible is to confront reversal again and again. As one of us has written elsewhere, "At the crucial moments when God displayed his mighty acts in history to reveal his nature and will, God *also* intervened to liberate the poor and oppressed."[5] The moments of intervention are also moments of reversal, moments when what one might expect is not what one gets, when those the world deems insignificant prove to be precisely the ones the Creator of the world deems important.

The Story in the Bible

Reversal is evident in each of three crucial moments: the exodus, the destruction and captivity of Israel and Judah, and the incarnation.[6] The story of the exodus is the story of what happens to a ragtag band of slaves who moan and groan about their miserable existences in much of the biblical record. They are ruled by pharaohs whose characters must have formed the basis for the portrayal of Nurse Ratchett, and there is little reason to expect that much will happen to these people other than their enduring lives of vacant servitude before they disappear into the dim recesses of a history dominated by the powerful.

Then along comes Moses, a somewhat blemished figure of a savior, who killed one of the oppressing Egyptians and hid his body, and who had a long argument with God in which he implied that God was foolish to choose a stuttering fellow like him to lead his people out of slavery. But blemished leader and unlikely candidates for liberation come together, and, as if on a fishing boat heading out to sea, they elude Pharaoh and sail forth to make one of the larger marks on history any people have made. This is reversal enough, but the biblical text goes farther and claims that in such an event as this the nature of the Story God is telling is revealed. One of the central creedal texts of the Old Testament puts it this way:

> A wandering Aramean was my father; and he went down into Egypt and sojourned there, few in number; and there he became a nation, great, mighty, and populous. And the Egyptians treated us harshly, and afflicted us, and laid upon us hard bondage. Then we cried to the LORD the God of our fathers, and the LORD heard our voice, and saw our affliction, our toil, and our

oppression; and the LORD brought us out of Egypt with
a mighty hand and an outstretched arm, with great
terror, with signs and wonders.

(Deuteronomy 26:5–8)

And so the Israelites experienced reversal as a hopeful
and liberating ingredient in their Story. But the time came
when they, now having in many ways changed roles in the
Story, now having become rich and powerful, now able to
play the role of Nurse Ratchett, experienced reversal as
warning and judgment. Now divided into two kingdoms,
Israel and Judah, they were warned by prophets from both
kingdoms that unless they changed their ways reversal was
once again imminent. By Amos, by Hosea, by Micah, by
Jeremiah and more they were warned that one day God
would take the unlikely ones, the excluded ones, the ones
staring vacantly in the mental hospitals, and would make of
them a new nation: "In that day, says the LORD, I will assem-
ble the lame and gather those who have been driven away"
(Micah 4:6).

As the Story enters its New Testament phase, the theme
of reversal only strengthens. Who are the villains in that
part of the Story, asks Buechner, but the ones "who more
often than not wear the fancy clothes and go riding around
in sleek little European jobs marked Pharisee, Corps Di-
plomatique, Legislature, Clergy." Who are the heroes, "the
ones who stand a chance of being saved by God because
they know they don't stand a chance of being saved by
anybody else? They go around looking like the town whore,
the village drunk, the crook from the IRS."[7] Then there is
the one who

> has no form or comeliness. His clothes are what he
> picked up at a rummage sale. He hasn't shaved for
> weeks. He smells of mortality. We have romanticized
> his raggedness for so long that we can catch echoes
> only of the way it must have scandalized his time in the
> horrified question of the Baptist's disciples, "Are *you*
> he who is to come?" (Matt. 11:13); you with pants that
> don't fit and a split lip; in the black comedy of the sign
> they nailed over his head where the joke was written
> out in three languages so nobody would miss the
> laugh.[8]

Without comeliness he is, yes; and that stimulates one set of expectations. But then comes the great reversal: "The whole point of the fairy tale of the Gospel is, of course, that he is king in spite of everything."[9] He is king, and his mission as summed up in his inaugural message reverses what one expects great leaders to say at such a time. No thundering about weakness vis-à-vis the Romans or the Russians, no calls for good Jews or Americans to sit tall in the saddle once more. No: "The Spirit of the Lord is upon me, because he has anointed me to preach good news to the poor" (Luke 4:18–19).

Furthermore, Christian faith affirms, Jesus uniquely mediates the Story God is telling, and one thing is clear. The Story is rife with reversal. And at this point in our recapping of the Story it seems safe to say that the reversals are not just any kind, but ones predictable in their unpredictability. Mary's Magnificat summarizes it well: God has "scattered the proud" and has "put down the mighty from their thrones." Those of "low degree" and the hungry have been exalted and filled, while the rich have been "sent empty away" (Luke 1:51–53).

The Story According to Liberation Theology

This reversal is one of the truths held dear by liberation theology, which has arisen from the suffering of the poor and oppressed and attempts to speak to that suffering. Liberation theologians care about many things, but certainly one of the things they care most deeply about is the communication of the inescapable thread of reversal running through the biblical Story. They believe, and rightly so, that the Story is most accessible to those who are in a position to experience reversal as a joyous event. Justo L. Gonzalez and Catherine G. Gonzalez put it well:

> God has a proclivity for speaking the word through the powerless. The whole Bible bears witness to this. Is this an accident, or is it an essential element of the gospel itself? Is there something about God's word that can best be heard and spoken by the powerless? Liberation theology would say there is indeed. . . . The powerful have a difficult time hearing God accurately. Their choice seems to be hearing God's word to them

through some apparently powerless person—Nathan, Amos, Simon Peter, Jesus—or not hearing it at all.[10]

This is a harsh truth for those of us who are powerful to hear, this truth that God is, in effect, on the side of the poor and oppressed against the unjust rich and the exploitative powerful. Yet there may be hope even for us who experience this reversal of expectations—this shattering realization that the God we thought was on our side may in fact be against us. Beyond the first reversal, the reversal that would come if our power or prestige or wealth were stripped from us, there could come a second reversal—the realization that what we always thought we needed was, in fact, oppressing us. The Gonzalezes speak to this, noting that the white male preacher, who may often find himself in this category of the powerful, can "discover how the system that oppresses the black, the Hispanic, the native American, and the woman, also oppresses him."[11]

Key Issues

In Chapter 6 we will address further this matter of how we experience reversal and how this might affect our preaching. For now let it be noted again that we are assuming the principle of reversal to be a crucial one in approaching the issues from a perspective faithful to the biblical point of view. Keeping that in mind, and adding to it our concern that the multidimensionality of the issues be respected, we want to turn now to an examination of how our various concerns apply to specific issues.

As we turn in that direction, however, we want to make clear what we will *not* attempt to do. For one thing, in the few pages we can devote to each issue, we will not provide a comprehensive guide to matters so complex that countless books and articles have examined their intricacies. We will simply treat each issue like a nut and try to crack it open just enough that some of the meat of preaching possibilities may be glimpsed inside. In the Appendix we suggest places the preacher might turn to gain greater understanding of the issues.

As we work through these issues, we will be keeping in mind the interior, personal, structural, and transcendent dimensions and the principle of reversal. We will not, however, attempt to give equal treatment to each ingredient in dealing with every issue. The transcendent dimension, particularly, will remain largely in the background. There are two reasons for this. First, reversal and transcendence are often interconnected in our approach; thus our "reversed" perspective is rooted in our faith that there is a dimension to our Story that gives it odd and unexpected and—ultimately—divine twists. Second, what we have already said about transcendence in general will often be applicable without much change to specific issues.

We will also be keeping in mind, without much explicit reference, what we have said about the church. The church, we assume, is the context in which the new realities a preacher hopes to stimulate can be first made flesh. Even in the church the flesh may only begin to cover the bones, to make visible the outlines of a new humanity. But it is there that the plot these new humans are trying to live out is likely to become visible first; from there it can spread.

These are the issues we have chosen to examine: abortion, economic justice, human rights, the earth, and war and violence. There are other, perhaps equally important issues. We have chosen these five because they are among the most pervasive and inescapable of the issues and will have to be faced by any preacher who tries to deal with matters of national or international import.

Abortion

We have chosen abortion as an issue worthy of examination for two reasons. First, especially since the 1973 Supreme Court decision legalizing abortion, it refuses to go away; any preacher about social concerns who succeeds in avoiding it risks looking very much like an ostrich. Second, abortion is often dealt with one-dimensionally. Some worry about the issue mainly at the personal level and what happens to fetus or mother. Some focus on the interior dimension and the mother's psychological state. Others take aim at government policy with little regard—whether they defend or oppose abortion—for how abstract policy finally works itself out in specific situations.

Since preaching easily falls prey to the same flattening of

perspective, we want to look at ways a multidimensional approach may lessen that tendency. While we have a bias (against abortion except when the physical life of the mother is threatened), our concern is not so much to argue a position as to model how one might work through the issue. Those who dislike our conclusions can, we hope, still benefit from our process.

The principle of *reversal* is an appropriate entry point to the issue, since it immediately asks us to put on biblical spectacles and ponder the matter from the peculiar angle of vision provided by the biblical Story. To do so will not so sharpen vision that no obscuring haze remains. There is no one proof text that settles the matter. At the same time, the Bible does seem to point in the direction of the fetus being a person,[12] giving it potentially the same right to life as any person. One will not want to reject this possibility too quickly, for when one enters the realm of reversal which is the biblical Story, things are not always what they seem; things are turned topsy-turvy; the unexpected may be precisely what one should expect. In this case the potential importance of even a tiny fertilized egg cannot be ignored. One can then use that insight as guide through the various dimensions of the issue.

That insight may help one find a way through the maze of arguments, biases, and influences that comprise abortion's *structural* dimension. Among broad structural forces that impinge on the issue are economic concerns, which can in turn shape social values. If aborting the fetus of a poor mother is cheaper than putting a child on the welfare rolls once it is born, or if aborting the deformed fetus is cheaper than providing care for a handicapped person,[13] then it becomes very tempting to opt for the cheaper outcome, particularly in a society that likes affluence and tends to choose its values based on the price tag. The principle of reversal counteracts this. It suggests that precisely what seems less valuable may be a jewel of great price, including the baby with Down's syndrome and that child who, instead of being aborted because she resulted from her mother's rape, grew into Ethel Waters and sang of the One whose eye is even on the sparrow.[14]

The preacher who takes this dimension into account will thus be providing an alternate framework of values in which wrestling with the issue at the *personal* level can take place. This is the level at which specific women and men and a fetus and perhaps other children (if a family is involved) are affected. Preaching aimed at this dimension can help those wrestling with abortion to keep in mind that what is expedient is not always what is right or even what will ultimately bring the greatest joy. In this odd tale which is our Story, who can be sure that the decision to eradicate a fetus that seems likely to bring only pain or inconvenience will not have been a decision to extinguish an unexpected joy (though it may, in fact, bring terrible pain, which the preacher also must admit)?

This is borne out as one examines the implications of abortion for the *interior* dimension. According to one study, 92 percent of mothers and 82 percent of fathers of fetuses that were aborted on medical grounds later suffered depression.[15] And there are indications that those who would have been siblings of a fetus had it not been aborted suffer trauma because they fear parental love is conditional.[16] However, at the same time as such findings may help the preacher identify the possible interior results of abortion, they should also stimulate the offering of grace, not judgment, to those who have, for whatever reasons, chosen abortion.

To deal with the interior dimension is also to deal not only with the emotional impact of abortion on those involved but also with the ways in which larger cultural values create interior dynamics, interior motivations, and drives and insecurities that are difficult to escape. Thus part of the preacher's task is to highlight ways in which people's interior dynamics change as their lives are rooted in the alternate reality which the Story calls us all to live out, and as they then long, not for lives untroubled by pain and inconvenience, but for lives filled with the hope that God can use pain and inconvenience to move the Story forward.

Economic Justice

Reversal plays a role in economic justice. We do not want to romanticize those oppressed by economic injustice. Poor and hungry people are precisely that, poor and hungry, and their condition is not to be celebrated. They are also, like all people, broken, and not by virtue of their condition exempt from sin. Nevertheless, to be oppressed is to be *potentially* more open to God than are the rich and comfortable. Richard Batey says:

> Beginning with the experience that the poor were often oppressed by the wicked rich, the poor were considered to be the special objects of Yahweh's protection and deliverance (Pss. 9:18; 12:5). . . . Therefore the poor looked to Yahweh as the source of deliverance from enemies and oppressors. This attitude of trust and dependence exemplified that piety that should have characterized every Israelite. In this way the concept of the "pious poor" developed.[17]

The poor, being more nakedly dependent on God, are potentially more open to God. They are potentially closer to understanding the plot of God's Story than are the comfortable, happy enough in the stories they have the power to spin for themselves that they may not care whether or not a larger Story is being told. This sets the stage for a startling reversal: the rich, the powerful, the rulers, those who manage the forces creating the net of injustice in which the poor and hungry are caught, think *they* are the heroic figures of the day. Instead, according to the Story, if there are to be heroes they may be the least expected ones, from among the poor and hungry.

This reversal tells us preachers that we (if facing a congregation of largely comfortable people) will be approaching the issue from the wrong end if we view our task as stimulating the good people in front of us to be nicer when possible to the less fortunate. Our first task, instead, is to help such people (and ourselves!) realize we are less good than we have thought. As we sit in our soft pews, thinking it is we who hold the power to move the Story forward by helping the poor, the Story may be unfolding most dramatically in the midst of the poor. It may be *they* who hold the greater power to move the Story forward and to help us find our role in it.

This startling possibility can be explored in every dimension. To apply it to the *interior* dimension is to help one's listeners face the pain groaning within them underneath the gloss of satisfaction which affluence often allows them to paint over hurt. It is gently but surely to help them confront the fact that sometimes they rush and run and buzz with business because they don't want to face the void inside, the soul restless until it rests in God.

This exposing of need sets the stage for the appearance of wise ones to point the way out of the void. Key among the wise ones are the poor whose pain has opened them to God, those guides emerging in places like the inner cities of the United States and in El Salvador, Nicaragua, the Philippines, South Africa. They are the wise because they are the ones used to facing God in the midst of the elemental realities of life. They know better than the comfortable how to navigate the highways and byways of the journey toward God.

The Gonzalezes give an example, noting that when the powerful interact with Luke's account of Jesus proclaiming release to the captives, they tend to identify with Jesus, and to edge toward a dangerous messianism. The powerless, on the other hand, hear in that same text a promise of release.[18] They may thus be among the ones who can guide the comfortable into facing their buried brokenness, so that in facing their hidden need for salvation they can at last experience to their core the goodness of the news Jesus offers.

As such internal transformation is stimulated, it will also be important to work at *personal* transformation. Rubem Alves, writing from Brazil, has "a practical suggestion": instead of turning all our celebrations, such as Christmas, into times when we celebrate our excess and so strengthen the walls separating us from those who have nothing, "it would be possible to start an opposite movement: the churches could create celebrations based on poverty. Christmas: occasion on which, in Christian homes, meals are eaten with the poor."[19]

Adopting such a suggestion would weaken the walls separating poor from comfortable, but they wouldn't fall down without some intentional marching around the city of Jericho! If the walls *are* to crumble, we comfortable ones will have to wrestle with what it means to live in such a way that we can identify with the poor, not just for the sake of the poor, but for our own sake. This may include opting for downward mobility. It may mean making career decisions

not on the basis of salary but on the basis of their compati-
bility with a Story intent on making heroes of the downtrodden. It may mean choosing simpler life-styles, not only so
that there will be more resources to go around but also
because the simpler life is likely to be more in touch with
the plot of the Story than a life so cushioned it can't thrill
to the Story's austere yet joyful plot.[20]

As preaching highlights the personal and interior trans-
formations that can occur, it opens the way for a new understanding of the *structural* dynamics that feed economic injustice. The preacher will not want to impose dogmatic
political opinions on parishioners. But the preacher *will*
want to offer a clear enough, reversal-tinged perspective,
that parishioners, whatever their notions of how that perspective translates into hard political realities, will be
guided by it: As they vote and write to Congress. As they
choose which corporate products to patronize. As they
make their own decisions in those structures they influence,
such as businesses. As they choose to live out the Story's
and not the world's plot.

Human Rights

In every country or society some persons are denied full
access to dignity, to respect, to participation in the life of
the dominant group. Sometimes, not only are persons denied access to such rights, but their rights are taken from
them by torture or imprisonment. Such denial of rights,
whether passive or active, is a disease that respects few
ideological boundaries. The Soviet Union and the regimes
it backs deny rights to Jews and to dissidents who refuse to
toe the Communist Party line; the United States has yet to
give full access to dignity and power to many of its minority
groups and has often backed repressive regimes, as in Iran,
Nicaragua, the Philippines.

How is one to preach meaningfully and accessibly about
yet one more labyrinthine social issue—human rights? It
will come as no surprise that we make *reversal* our entry
point. Reversal suggests that anywhere one catches sight of
rights denied, there one might want to look for clues to the
unfolding of the Story. Where a person, group, or characteristic of a group is being ridiculed, repressed, or killed,

there one may find a guiding truth the destroyers need to face but are doing their best to avoid. This may be true in the case of women, whose situation we will briefly probe as an example of how one might approach any group suffering from loss of rights.

Around the world, wherever patriarchal values have held sway, women have been secondary characters. In preaching about rights for women, as is the case with the poor, it may not be enough for the preacher to reach out a patronizing hand to help women step up to equality with men. That is part of the issue—for women to gain access to rights and privileges and status formerly reserved for men, for women to receive equal pay for equal work, for women to be included in language.

But reversal suggests there may be more. It may be that women have some guiding to do, that they need not only to be given *access* to the male world but to be allowed to *lead* the world, whether male or female, in those areas where they have been pioneers. We mean by this not necessarily that women have pioneered because of genes or hormones or some sort of special "feminine" nature, though the question of gender-specific differences is still being studied. We speak, rather, of the insight they have been forced to develop as relatively powerless people.

The preacher grappling with the issue of rights for women will want to explore and apply this insight at all levels. Rosemary Radford Ruether, exploring links between feminism and peace, notes ways this might be done:

> Feminism fundamentally rejects the power principle of domination and subjugation. It rejects the concept of power which says that one side's victory must be the other side's defeat. Feminism must question social structures based on this principle at every level.[21]

Ruether goes on to note some of the levels. Speaking of the *personal* dimension, she says that feminism must question "the competition of men and women in personal relationships." And at the *structural* level, feminism must question "the competition of the nations of the globe, including the U.S. and the U.S.S.R."[22] She doesn't explicitly deal with the *interior* dimension, but questioning the power principle of domination at other levels will have its impact within. As

persons orient their lives toward interdependence rather
than independence, they become more willing to express
emotion, to be tender, to face their hurts and fears and
depths in the confidence that others are not so much com-
petitors to be defended against as friends reaching out healing hands to inner hurts. They become better able, in other
words, to live out the Story, which values precisely this
offering up of lives to each other rather than the hoarding
of life for the sake of self.

Then Ruether wraps the dimensions together in this vision:

> We seek an alternative power principle of empowering
> in community rather than power over and disabling of
> others. Such enabling . . . is based on a recognition of
> the fundamental interconnectedness of life, of men and
> women, blacks and whites, Americans and Nicara-
> guans, Americans and Russians, humans and the non-
> human community of animals, plants, air, and water.[23]

That is the kind of vision the preacher on human rights
will want to instill. Such a vision will not only affirm each
human's right to dignity and access to the dominant group's
prerogatives; it will understand that the outcast may be a
heroine or hero in disguise, carrier of unsuspected truth.

The Earth

Ruether's questioning of domination in relation to
human interaction with the nonhuman leads naturally into
a discussion of the earth, our physical home, our environment, and how one might preach about that. The power
principle of domination has guided our treatment of the
earth, and we are beginning to sense the result. A terrible
reversal—in the form not of eucatastrophe but of bad catastrophe—may be building; we who thought we controlled
the earth may find ourselves controlled by it as the earth
rises up to tell us it is a more important player in our Story
than we want to admit.

Scientists, environmentalists, government regulators,
and industry representatives squabble ceaselessly over exactly what is happening to the earth. Not many lowly
preachers can claim certitude in this area; we authors cer-

tainly do not. Neither, however, can the preacher ignore the potential for disaster. No preacher knows exactly what toxic wastes, acid rain, rain-forest destruction, soil erosion, and more will do to the earth. But any preacher who cares about the earth will want to note the possibility that toxic wastes will increasingly threaten the drinking water of millions; that acid rain may kill the forests; that as rain forests die, climactic shifts may take place, perhaps turning parts of fertile America into wasteland; that topsoil can only trickle off farmland for so long before it is gone; that the chemicals we use in refrigerators and air conditioners to cool our food and ourselves may be tearing great holes in that protective atmospheric tent which is ozone.

Having established, through such a survey of *structural* dynamics, that a problem does exist, a preacher might want to ask what the Story says about how the problem came to be and how it might be resolved. Such questioning might suggest that the Story itself has led to the problem. Genesis 1:28 says that after creating man and woman, God "blessed them, and God said to them, 'Be fruitful and multiply, and fill the earth and subdue it; and have dominion over . . . every living thing that moves upon the earth.' " There are those who believe the appropriation of such verses by the Judeo-Christian tradition and Western culture in general has played a key role in creating the building ecological crisis.[24]

That may be true, but it seems to us that it is not the Bible but its misuse that is at fault. Genesis 1 speaks to a pre-fall situation; it assumes that those exercising dominion will do so in the context of the boundaries symbolized by the prohibition against eating of the fruit of the tree of the knowledge of good and evil (Gen. 2:16–17). Dominion happens in submission to God's dream of an earth in which all are threads in a delicately interconnected ecosystem, dancing joyfully together around the tree of life symbolizing their submission to God as the center of their existences.

But humanity is fallen, and so when God walks in the garden in the cool of the day to see what beauties humanity's gentle dominion has created, God sees instead a place of shame. The river Euphrates flows turgid with waste; the acid rain drips like tears off the leaves of the tree of life; a few crippled animals limp by—the rest are extinct.

The preacher will want to address this truth that our style of dominion is not God's style. All of us need to face our own complicity in what happens when fallenness twists good stewardship into rape. This has two implications for the *interior* dimension. First, the preacher can suggest that what goes on within, the ever-present temptation toward hubris, toward overweening pride, contributes to environmental destruction. One way to begin the process of healing the earth is to choose metanoia, a turning from the false center of self to the true center of God so that the behaviors that impinge upon the earth will take place more nearly in the context of God's original purposes for creation.

A second implication is this: shivering within many, along with justifiable guilt, is the fear which produces psychic numbing. If, as seems possible, within a few generations the earth may be barely able to support human life, then a sadness too great to bear threatens to overwhelm us at any moment. That blue sky shining on crisp red and golden leaves in fall may not glow too much longer. The preacher needs to make such fears as bearable as possible, partly just by articulating them and letting people feel them in a supportive environment, and partly by extending the hope that if enough people touch their sadness, all is not lost.

After the preacher helps such sadness and such hope to be expressed, she or he can add a further hope: the experts who say the earth is in trouble also say that no one knows what capacities for healing the earth may yet demonstrate. And there lingers the great hope that a *transcendent* God still holds the world in the hands that created it. That hope may catalyze the release of energy in the *personal* dimension as people commit themselves to recycling, to life-styles minimizing consumption and trash production, to farming methods minimizing soil loss. Some may feel called to become advocates of broad *structural* changes caused by litigation or new government policies or altered economies that respect rather than exploit the good earth.

War and Violence

Perhaps it has always seemed that way, but surely it is no less true these days—that war and violence are mounting, like water climbing ever higher, to form a tidal wave that could sweep across the earth. From all levels flow the waters of destruction: From within each human heart, seething with its demons. From interpersonal relationships gone sour. From the spats, the posturings, the big and little wars spilling out across the nations. From the missiles and the bombs. From the fallout of all the issues we have been discussing, as poverty and oppression and torture call forth violence from the downtrodden, bringing down violence upon them from their oppressors.

How is a preacher to preach with the crest of that wave trembling over the congregation? It is hard to know. The Story seems a feeble thing to throw at forces like these raging across the earth. But it is all we preachers have, in the end, and if we don't think it is enough, then we had better sit down and stop pretending we have much to say. Perhaps our weapon is stronger than we first think, a pebble against Goliath, but a pebble, surely enough. What the preacher has to say is that, yes, war and violence threaten to overcome the world, but underneath unfolds a Story whose plot, as it is lived out, sends forth its own healing rivulets and ripples.

While it is difficult to know at which level the preacher might most effectively begin to stimulate such streams of peace to flow, it may be hard to communicate meaningfully about peace in other dimensions if persons have not begun to take off the blinders within, if they have not begun to work at peace in the *interior* dimension. In comments about the monk's vocation, but more broadly applicable, Thomas Merton says people need to face the darkness within if they are ultimately to heal the darkness without. Contemplative prayer, the turning within, is

> precisely the monk's chief service to the world: this silence, this questioning, this humble and courageous exposure to what the world ignores about itself—both good and evil. . . . The monk confronts his own humanity and that of his world at the deepest and most central point where the void seems to open out into black despair.[25]

To help listeners face their internal contribution to the powers of destruction, to help them face their violent shadows and in the facing help transmute the shadows so they can send forth rays of hope—that is a crucial part of the preacher's task as she or he deals with the issue of war and violence. But that is only part of the task. For Merton, as for us, true inner transformation leads inexorably to external change; that external change deepens internal growth, and the cycle continues.[26] Peace within contributes to peace without, and vice versa. The preacher will want to identify these interconnections and point the way not only toward inner peace but toward peace in the *personal* dimension. Thus the issue of war and violence will be seen to have an impact at the level of how the neighbor, the family member, the fellow Christian, the fellow worker, are treated.

It will then need to be remembered that personal interaction affects and is affected by the dynamics of the *structural* dimension. If waters of peace flow from interpersonal relationships while waters of destruction flow from votes in favor of more arms and yet more warheads and a policy favoring force over diplomacy, the two work at cross-purposes. The effect is like the turbulence that erupts when a river emptying into the sea from one direction encounters the waves crashing in from the other. Sermons dealing with the structural level will help listeners see the total picture, and nudge them toward a vision of more-than-private peace.

And then, woven through it all, ought to flow the spine-tingling twists in the Story that relate to war and violence and all the other issues that feed into it.

According to our understanding of the Story, the theme of *Christus Victor,* of Christ triumphant over the powers of evil and even the power of war and violence, is a crucial one. But it is also crucial to note the *way* in which that triumph is accomplished. Jesus resists all temptation to bring in God's kingdom through lethal force.[27] As he lives his life and preaches about the nature of life in the kingdom he calls for an end to policies of retaliation (an eye for an eye) in favor of policies of peace, policies that cut apart the cycle of violence (love your enemies).

Now we modern preachers try, along with our parishioners, to wriggle our way as best we can out of the difficulties that kind of vision poses for hard-headed realism. What does Jesus' simple peasant style have to do with a world waiting for the tidal wave to crash? We tend to gear our preaching toward encouraging a few little adjustments here and there that seem feasible—being nicer to our spouses, at least. Certainly we must take the complex realities into account. But it is sad indeed when in so doing we miss the heart of the Story and the hope it holds out for us.

Jesus not only preaches the vision, he dies for it. Here another dimension, the *transcendent* one, appears; and it appears intertwined with the ingredient of *reversal.* Jesus dies, but on the third day the grave lies empty, and with the living Jesus at its head the movement that will sweep the world begins: Eucatastrophe. The hand of God. And reversal. If God is to act at all in bringing in the kingdom, one would expect it to be by strengthening an army of noble warriors ready to sweep away the evil foe. Instead, victory comes through the least expected means—a mangled body dangling on the symbol of shame which was the cross.

The preacher dealing with war and violence needs most fundamentally to communicate the assurance that as Christians faithfully live for peace at every level of their lives, the Story, if the past twists in its plot mean anything at all, adds their faithfulness to its forward movement. The rivers of peace thunder forth and the winds of God blow, and some-day—even if it takes countless Christians going to their own deaths with Jesus, giving up their lives rather than fighting to bring in the kingdom—what looks so perilously like defeat will be turned back, and the tidal wave will be one not of destruction but of healing waters.

4

Building a Biblical House
of Being

In this chapter we want to broaden our definition of what
it means to preach about social concerns. Such preaching
addresses specific social issues. It can also do more: John R.
W. Stott helps us understand that as he argues for the
development of the "Christian mind," which

> is not a mind . . . thinking about specifically Christian
> or even religious topics, but a mind which is thinking
> about everything, however apparently "secular," and
> doing so "Christianly" or within a Christian frame of
> reference. It is not a mind stuffed full with pat answers
> to every question, all neatly filed as in the memory bank
> of a computer; it is rather a mind which has absorbed
> biblical truths and Christian presuppositions so
> thoroughly that it is able to view every issue from a
> Christian perspective and so reach a Christian judg-
> ment about it.[1]

For the preacher, stimulating the development of a particular mind, of a particular perspective or worldview or
structure of thinking and being, is as important as sharing
conclusions about specific issues. This is not to say that
specific positions should never be taken. It *is* to say that
preaching about social concerns includes not only guiding
people toward specific stances but also giving them the
resources to arrive at such stances on their own. It involves
helping them build a structure of being from which prophetic understandings of issues will naturally flow.

How preaching might help build such a structure is what

we now want to explore. We will look first at what guidance the Bible gives us in the matter, at what kind of structure emerges in the pages of the Bible, and of what materials it is built. Then we will investigate ways we might enter and dwell within the biblical structure today. Finally we will examine how preaching that is geared toward building such a structure, rather than focusing on specific social issues, might nevertheless release catastrophic—or, their result being to create rather than to destroy—*eucatastrophic* forces in the social arena.

The Biblical House of Being and Its Building Blocks

In this section we want to examine the kind of structure we find in the Bible. First we want to consider what blocks are used to build it, which will include taking a closer look at such by now familiar topics as story and multidimensionality and the less familiar topic of myth.

The Building Blocks

We have already touched on many of the Bible's structural building blocks, its stones, its bricks, its girders. Now we want to examine them in more detail and with more of an eye toward the totality they build. The key blocks continue to be story and the dimensions and ingredients it encompasses.

Story

Story is not simply an interesting but discardable building block dreamed up by writers who happen to like stories and think they can make sermons more palatable; it is instead a central stone, the keystone without which attempts to grasp the outlines of the biblical structure risk collapse.

Amos Wilder has been a central figure in the movement to recover the Bible's narrative core. Wilder notes that the narrative mode is not unique to the Bible, present as it is in much of the literature of many religions. He argues, however, that "the narrative mode is uniquely important in Christianity" (though much of the story is important also to Judaism, which of course shares a large portion of the Bible with Christianity). Wilder points out that if one turns from

the Bible to "other religious and philosophical classics the
story aspects may be relatively marginal. Their sacred books
may often rather take the form of philosophical instruction
or mystical treatise or didactic code or oracular vision."[2]
But a Christian, says Wilder,

> can confess his faith wherever he is, and without his
> Bible, just by telling a story or a series of stories. It is
> through the Christian story that God speaks, and all
> heaven and earth come into it. God is an active and
> purposeful God and his action with and for men has a
> beginning, a middle, and an end like any good story.
> The life of a Christian is not like a dream shot through
> with visions and illuminations, but a pilgrimage, a race,
> in short, a history. The new Christian speech inevitably
> took the form of a story. The believers wanted to tell
> the world the way of the world as they saw it.[3]

Elizabeth Achtemeier echoes this, noting that the Bible
does not primarily *tell* such central truths as that God is
love; it is not primarily a compendium of dogmatic statements or legalistic demands or propositional summaries;
the Bible, instead, *shows* the truth, offering stories unfolding
through pictures, through images, through actions. God's
love, says Achtemeier, "is defined by a story—of a supper
in an upper room and a friend's betrayal; of a prayer and
a kiss, and a mob in a garden. . . . Love is pictured through
the events of a whipping, a trial, a mocking, and a crown of
thorns, and finally by a cross and nails."[4]

Multidimensionality
An associated building block is the one we discussed in
chapter 2: *multidimensionality,* or, to use Wilder's term, "holism." What that means, says Wilder, is that the Bible has a
broad "scope of awareness," one that encompasses "the
multi-dimensional reality and realism, the inclusion of private and public, of the inner life and the social-historical, of
somatic and visionary, of ethical and metaphysical."[5]
The Bible, suggests Wilder, contains narrative cycles constructed both of story and multidimensionality: "We find
one or another kind of overarching plot from beginnings to
fulfillment [story], and . . . a very dense portrayal of the
human experience and existence in all its empirical reality

[multidimensionality]." That part of the Story found in the Old Testament, for instance, grew over the years, era by era and strand by strand. Finally it emerged as the great epic we read today, the saga of creation and fall, of the patriarchs and the exodus and the entry into the Promised Land, and also of sadness and exile and the yearning for a better day ahead.[6]

Myth

One of the ways the Bible conveys this multidimensionality, this holism, is through a form of story one might call *myth.* The very mention of the word "myth" sends warning flags flying for many. We use it reluctantly, not wanting it to mean what some take it to mean: a fanciful fable or timeless, ahistorical account. We use it in much the same sense as we earlier used the term "fairy" story—meaning, in the case of the biblical Story, a tale which seems fanciful and fabulous but also happens to be true. We use it, despite reservations, so we can dialogue with sources who use it— though with the provision that we endorse only that portion of a source's viewpoint we explicitly affirm.

We do not, in the modern world, experience very often and directly the mythic form of story. A newspaper account, the average novel, the latest movie, are usually not mythical, unfolding as they do within our modern perspective that we are living in a "horizontal" world, in a "one-level empirical reality."[7] By and large, we do not experience our journey through life as a mythical one but as a rather banal progression through wearyingly familiar stages of the life cycle, at the end of which we die, like the grass and the trees and the bees.

The Bible, on the other hand, throbs with myth. There are many technical definitions of what that means, but for our purposes we will stick with Wilder, who says that myth in the Bible is to be "understood . . . in the sense of total world-representation, involving, of course, not only what we would call the external cosmos but man as well, and all in the light of God."[8] Myth in the Bible serves to convey both what it means to live and move and have being, and simultaneously in whom it is that we live and move and have our being. It is the telling of rich and complex stories penetrated by and unfolding against the backdrop of the divine itself.

The story of creation and fall is such a myth. What that means can perhaps be suggested by contrasting the biblical account with contemporary secular treatments of related matters. Among theories of the beginning of the universe is the "big bang" theory. Billions of years ago there occurred a primordial explosion, among whose by-products was the planet Earth. Eventually from the ooze crawled forth grotesque creatures, which over millions of years transmuted into human beings. Now here we are, not quite sure exactly what we're here for, and not all that ready to consider ourselves fallen, since we have, after all, come a long way from the swamps.

Such a description hopelessly oversimplifies scientific thought and edges toward caricature. That may be misleading, because we are not trying to reject secular understandings, which offer valid insight. We are merely trying to draw a contrast between the realms of secular and biblical understandings. Secular investigations of reality tend to take place within the "one-level empirical reality," the dimension of empirically verifiable cause and effect, the level of description rather than meaning, of "what" rather than "why."

What the Bible does with creation and fall is something radically different. God broods over the face of the deep. Then God begins to tell a Story, and God creates a physical setting for the Story, complete with all the things the setting needs to make it livable. God populates the setting with all kinds of running, leaping, walking, crawling, and dancing living things. Then the Storyteller creates characters to dwell within the setting and live out the Story. But their Teller has told them that if they want the plot to be a happy one, they will have to recognize that any good plot and any self-respecting character has to have some limits, some boundaries. A plot without limits is no plot and a character without boundaries soon ceases to be recognizable. So here are the limits, here is a boundary, says the Teller: You may not eat of the tree of the knowledge of good and evil. But they eat, they violate the boundaries, and the plot goes awry and their lives come undone.

The part of the Story found in Genesis 1–3 is dense and complex. It unfolds on earth and in heaven. It comments on

its characters' physical environment and their relationship
to it. It describes their external actions and offers clues to
what is going on inside them. It communicates through
symbols and metaphors and images that fill the hearer with
pictures, pictures throbbing with color and detail and
movement.

It hints at why we walk the earth and why our walk is so
often a stumble and a crawl through a desolate wilderness,
and even why it may yet be that the last remaining few of
us will creep over a literal wilderness pitted and charred and
still smoking from blasts that tore the skin right off the
planet. It doesn't, though, *tell* us exactly that; it mainly *shows*
us that and weaves around our lives the structure of a Story
we still are living out. It is, in short, a myth, a Story gathering up the whole of the universe and the life within it and
unfolding it within the bosom of the divine.

What we mean by that, let us again be clear, is not that
myth tells us about something which stands above or apart
from history and the real world. We are not trying to say
that the mythical structure within which the Bible sees reality unfolding is one cut off from history and the real world.
History and myth need not be mutually exclusive. We *are*
saying that Genesis does not go about conveying truth in
the same way *The New York Times* does, giving primarily a
literal, detail-by-detail account of what happened at precisely what time on what day. The Genesis account is trying
to tell us much more than that on Day One, God brooded;
twenty-four hours later God said, "Let there be light!" and
at the end of a week, there it all was. At the same time,
Genesis *is* telling us about historical events. It is telling us
that as the Story has unfolded over the countless years, this
is *what* has been happening and this is *why* it has been
happening and this is *Who* has been making it happen. And
what the *Times* says has been happening is part of the Story,
but the *Times* can't grasp the half of it!

The House of Being

Story. Multidimensionality. Myth. What is the Bible trying to create with these strong building blocks, which encompass not only creation and fall but the whole majestic

sweep of the biblical Story, what Stott calls "the fourfold biblical scheme of creation, fall, redemption, and consummation"?[9]

There are a number of ways one could describe the structure the Bible builds. We have already mentioned Stott's "Christian mind." We could also suggest that the Bible offers the world a supporting *skeleton.* The Bible presents the outline of the world's story. It does not enfold within its pages the whole story; to accomplish that it would have to record every jot and tittle of all that has been, is, or ever will be. But sticking through its pages, sometimes with the spare and bony angularity skeletal structures are apt to have, *is* an outline, a sketchy but recognizable story. Without this Story outline, the world flops around uncertain where it came from, where it is going, or even if it came from or is going anywhere. With it, the world begins to firm up, to straighten its back, to find out where it came from and where it is going, and to stride purposefully forward.

With its Story outline, to put it another way, the Bible draws us a map. Amos Wilder suggests that the gridwork of the map is made up of all the "ancient patterns of rehearsal in the Bible," those intersecting highways and byways formed by the Israelite struggle to understand and live out the Story. Says Wilder:

> We can say that these ancient rehearsals may be recognized in some sort as the archetypal molds of our own histories and fabulations. In these tracks our own courses are run. . . . When we come into the world, in whatever century since, we find ourselves in a mystery that has been mapped, even if we disbelieve it, and even if the ancient chart has all but faded away. Nevertheless, our inmost being [carries] this imprint, suggested by such formulas as "lost and found," "from slave to royalty," and by such models as those of pilgrim, servant, saint.[10]

A third way of envisioning the structure present in the Bible, and the one we will focus on, because it provides an image conveying the kind of all-encompassing meaning we are looking for, is as "house of being," as Wilder puts it. Wilder says the biblical Story has served those described within the Bible and those caught up within its world in the millennia after as "a kind of cable or lifeline across the abysses of time and cultures, because man is here sustained over against anarchy, nonbeing and nescience."[11] In the midst of the chaos, the uncertainties, the potential meaninglessness of human existence, the Story builds a house—a place within which to find purpose and meaning, a place offering the stability and perspective needed to understand and weather the storms of history.

In the days after the collapse of Israel and Judah, for example, as the people groped through a dark time of collapsed hopes, lost meaning, and broken purpose—a time that hauntingly evokes our own—the Story served as a beacon in the night, as a refuge from the storm. Wilder says the Story offered, in a way nothing but story could, the hope that beyond "the recent apostasies and catastrophies" would come the time of "the renewal of the covenant in a restored Jerusalem."[12] The Story provided for the people a house of being when all the usual houses had been torn down, by remembering and telling what once was; by giving bearings to its hearers in the present moment through telling them where they were then; and by telling them where they were going and so offering hope for a future better than exile. Even in exile, perhaps especially in exile, now truly bereft of an earthly home, the people found within the Story their house of being.

That is what all the fuss about idolatry, all the suspicion of Baal and dangerous foreign influence which runs persistently through the Story, is about. That is what feeds the hesitancy to have kings like other nations. Idols and Baal and Caananite fertility rites and kings are all apt to tempt the people into deserting their true house of being in favor of houses whose safety is more tangible and whose pleasures and guarantees are more immediate.

Always against such bogus copies the Story vigorously protests, urging its characters to live only within its walls and no others. When its walls are trusted, they prove secure, precisely because, as we have been discussing, this is no thin and pallid Story, a Story about some ethereal reality its characters may someday enter. It is a dense and full-orbed Story, a Story that encompasses the ragged and the raw and the tormenting realities of life even as it strains toward a time when there will be tears no more.

What we are trying to get at here is that the Story offers something hard to find in modern life. It wrestles in an integrating way with what in the modern world is material given over to the psychologist, if it has to do with individuals or the psyche; to the sociologist, if it has to do with collective human behavior; to the scientist, if it has to do with the physical world; to the ethicist, if it has to do with questions of value; to the lawyer and the judge, if it has to do with justice; to the philosopher, if it has to do with matters of meaning; to the mystic, if it has to do with the ecstasies of the inner life.

Where in the modern world is the truly integrative vision, the house of being into which a person can enter to gain a unifying perspective? Different disciplines claim to offer that perspective, but they become instead new idols, bogus houses of being that can never fully satisfy. Modern preaching often perpetuates such disintegration. It allies itself with a particular field of modern endeavor and attempts to translate the biblical message into the assumptions of that field, and so offers only a biblicized but still ultimately secular perspective, rather than offering the primordial Story in all its richness.

We are not in any way opposed to attempts to relate the Story to the larger world or to the contributions that secular investigators have made to our understanding of the larger world. One of our main concerns, after all, has been to suggest that if the grandeur of the Story, with its multidimensional and mythopoetic elements, is properly grasped, it will be seen that the Story embraces all reality, whether sacred or profane, religious or secular.

When, therefore, someone like David Tracy calls for theology to speak to three audiences—church, academia (whether religious or not), and society at large—we applaud that call.[13] We are, however, concerned that conversation with the larger world is sometimes misdirected, that the church and its preachers sometimes allow the broader world to dictate what their agenda should be. Misdirected preachers see their task entirely as translating the Story into contemporary idioms.

Instead of psychology or sociology or a movie being used to clarify the contemporary meaning of the Story, the

Story's power is diluted in these vessels. The secular vessel takes the Story into itself and dominates instead of being taken into a Story which, though enriched by the vessel, does not allow it to control the direction of the discussion. When preachers relinquish their mythos, they allow the Story they are called to serve to melt away like ice on a summer day; they take some of the stones out of their house of being and leave holes through which the winter winds will blow when summer fades.

A Door Into the House of Being

If that is not to happen, we preachers are going to have to trust the Story more. We are going to have to be more willing to believe that the Bible does provide a safe and stout and satisfying house of being; one, moreover, large enough to take into itself the modern age—without breaking and proving itself sufficient only for the smaller, simpler world of days gone by.

How might such trust be fostered? What doors do we need to find and open so we can enter the biblical house of being and find our trust rewarded? There are at least two. One of them we want to save for our last chapter, where we will discuss the "hermeneutics of obedience," by which we mean the opening of a door into the biblical house that takes place when people decide to follow Jesus and live out the Story. Here we want to discuss another door, one that can be viewed from a variety of angles.

The Outlines of the Door

This door is not easy to delineate, partly because many are unsure just what its outlines are, and those who *are* sure sometimes contradict each other. The door has been called many things, not all of which necessarily refer to exactly the same reality, but all of which point in a similar direction. Among its names are these: the right side of the brain, the collective unconscious, "deep calling unto deep." What such names do not refer to seems clearer than what they do describe. They do not primarily refer to what might be called linear, logical thinking. They do not refer to the kind of intellectual process that is involved in communicating through intellectual abstractions and propositions.

Before we risk discussing what these terms *do* mean, we want to stress that we are not calling for the rejection of rationality, logic, linear thinking. Rational thinking is a precious gift. It is through incisive, critical thought that we test the hazier intuitions and feelings we are about to discuss. This book could not have been written without the gift of order and structure. We also want to be clear that the answer to the world's woes does not lie simply in more holistic styles of thinking or appropriating reality.[14]

If other modes of apprehending reality are used along with rationality to enter the biblical Story, that broader entry can open up great possibilities in the world. The reality God has created is a majestic one, and we need to use all the receptors of reality God has given us if we are to grasp even the dimmest outlines of the wonder in which we live and move. God's Spirit shares divine truth with us not only through our intellects but through our tears and laughter and shivers of intuition.

Fred B. Craddock says:

> Even though our society is often characterized as empiricist and scientific, individuals and groups still live in large measure by dreams, images, symbols, and myths. Teaching and preaching that stay in the conceptual world of ideas and doctrines, however true or right or current, leave hearers essentially unmoved. The consciousness in its imaginative depths is unaltered.[15]

Split-Brain Theory

What are those imaginative depths and how might they be reached? That is the key question, and that is where answers vary but still affirm a common core. Walter Wink's answer is that we process reality differently with the different hemispheres of our brain. The left side of the brain majors in the analytical, logical, abstract, sequential, cause-effect elements of our thinking. It senses time as moving from one point to another; it controls our use of speech, grammar, math. The right hemisphere controls the imaginative, holistic, noncausal aspects of our thinking. As we respond to art, to faces, to stories and images and symbols, to things in their wholeness rather than in part, or experience a sense of timelessness, we are using the right hemisphere.[16]

Wink's thesis is that our culture, with its bias toward one-dimensional acceptance of reality, values what is processed by the left side of the brain and devalues what is processed by the right side. This theory is controversial, and as studies in the area proceed, it is increasingly recognized that the relationship between left and right is intricate and complex. Neat divisions of labor are simplistic. Wink, acknowledging this, notes that what is, in the end, important is not so much how right and left brain function as that the full range of our ability to interact with reality be appropriated.[17]

The Collective Unconscious and Its Archetypes

Carl G. Jung approached the matter in another way, and understanding it requires knowing what he means by such terms as *collective unconscious* and *archetypes*. Both Sigmund Freud and Jung were pioneers in their theories of the unconscious, and Jung's work was partially dependent on Freud's. In Freud's view, there exists in each of our psyches an unconscious component made up of all those experiences, urges, or thoughts that have been repressed as too dangerous, unpleasant, painful, or anxiety-provoking. We are basically born with a clean slate, and our unconscious only develops through a lifelong process of repressing anxiety.[18]

Jung did not completely disagree. He called Freud's unconscious the *personal* unconscious and viewed it much as Freud did, though with some clear differences. But he also went one large step farther. June Singer says:

> Noting that similar images and myth motifs could be found in widely separated places all over the earth, and at different periods throughout the history of mankind, he came to a decisive insight: that *the unconscious is at its basis collective in character,* that is, composed of contents that are universal in their nature.[19]

For Jung, this collective unconscious is the deposit of all ancestral experience. Everything undergone by humanity since the beginning of time has in some way made its imprint and has helped create in all humans inherited predispositions governing ways of functioning, thinking, perceiving.[20]

Related to the concept of the collective unconscious is Jung's theory of archetypes. He says, "There are present in every psyche forms which are unconscious but nevertheless active—living dispositions . . . that preform and continually influence our thoughts and feelings and actions."[21] These archetypal forms, thought Jung, are present in each person's unconscious. They underlie the common mythological motifs Jung believed he had identified as he studied the mythology of cultures around the world. As he worked with his patients Jung was struck by the fact that he was able, or so he thought, to identify mythological motifs in their dreams, psychoses, and hallucinations that could only have erupted from an unconscious level participated in by all humanity. Jung came to this conclusion through observing that such motifs repeated mythological themes found elsewhere in the world to which the patients had not otherwise been exposed.[22]

Jung argued that archetypes, those dwellers in our depths and in the common depths of all humanity, operate at a preconceptual, precognitive, prerational level. A key archetype among the many he identified was that of the Self. The Self is that facet of our being which longs for and pulls us toward integration, wholeness; toward—ultimately—salvation. Among symbols representing it are the tree, calling to mind the tree of life.[23] When we respond to the story of creation and fall, with its archetypal symbols of tree of life as well as serpent, flaming sword, and more, we respond to them with our depths before we respond with our rational faculties.

As is the case with split-brain theory, Jung's approach has its detractors. Such concepts as the collective unconscious and archetypes may not be the best ways of clarifying the reality Jung was trying to investigate. And not all Jungian notions are compatible with Christian understandings. But at least they serve as analogies, as a way of thinking that helps keep us in touch with the possibility that we respond to life in broader and deeper and more mysterious ways than we are sometimes willing to admit.

Deep Calling Unto Deep

Amos Wilder is less concerned to develop sophisticated theories in this area, but (perhaps because of that) he offers some clarifying thoughts. He suggests that myths such as those of creation and fall convey truth which (though it can be cognitively grasped) grows out of more than the topsoil of rationality, however rich it may be. Such myths possess roots reaching deep down into the nutrients of our depths, however they may be perceived: "Whatever cognitive orientation a myth communicates is to be grasped by the same kind of imaginative apprehension that first shaped it, and only then transposed provisionally into conceptual statements."[24]

Speaking of the nativity texts, whose power has been lost for many, Wilder suggests that the problem may lie not so much with the Christmas story as with the inadequate "scale and compass of our responses, the quality of our answering imagination." The story of a baby born of overshadowed Mary in a stable with the hay and cow dung aims at our depths: "Deep speaks to deep." Our depths respond to the depths of the story.[25]

Wilder believes that we respond to life at the level of story, myth, archetype, before we respond with critical thought. Heart responds before brain. Yet brain tends to be all we bring to bear on biblical texts like the nativity stories. We miss the meaning that could grasp us if we could trust our hearts, our "affective and imaginative" depths.[26]

This happened to one of us when he tried to prepare a sermon on a nativity text and got bogged down in the critical details—apparent discrepancies between Matthew and Luke, the question of whether the virgin birth is intelligible to the modern mind. Meanwhile, "Away in a Manger" was playing on the record player, and his daughter, age two, danced slowly and intently, entranced by the quiet strains, the gentle beat, and the tender lyrics. As he watched, he realized she had caught the heart of the story, and his critical concerns, while important, were secondary to that heart.

Wilder tells of a similar experience he had as a teenager, an experience that has lingered—though he admits he may have been more susceptible to it because at the time he was young and working on a farm. He heard the parable of the sower expounded in "a rural Sunday school class taught by a village housewife," a context in which he no doubt received instruction that violated all the canons of proper biblical interpretation. And yet, he remembers, "I have always recalled with wonder the impact, the imaginative reverberations, and the psychic dynamics of the six verses of the parable."[27]

Wilder says that even though such intuitions have to be subjected to the checks and balances of critical thought, "over and above all rules and resources of interpretation later acquired, I had learned . . . to respect the naked text itself, to let the word and the words have their own untrammeled course, to be open to their deeper signals, to let . . . depth [speak] to depth."[28]

Such, then, is the shadowy outline of the door we are trying to investigate. We are trying, paradoxically, to clarify through reason something that tends to defy rational grasp, so we are not likely to attain more than a shadowy outline. Nevertheless, shadowy or not, there is truth here, truth with important implications for preaching. The truth is that we open the door into the biblical house of being not only by probing it with our mind but by approaching it with our entire being. Stories, images, and symbols spring from and are responded to by that part of our being which we describe through such metaphors as the right side of the brain, the collective unconscious and its archetypes, the deep, that ocean of intuition and feeling and apprehension of the numinous whose waves splash and crash within each one of us.

While we don't simply preach the naked text without interpretation, hoping to catalyze what Wilder experienced as a boy, neither will we want to strip the text too quickly of its original form, its original stories, myths, images, dreams, and symbols. Deep still calls to deep. In wondrous ways the Teller of our lives, and the Teller standing behind and inspiring the human tellers of the Bible's Story, works within us to open the door to the house of being.

Entering the House of Being

If we want to touch the entire being with our preaching, we will want to do what the Bible does; we will want often to show rather than simply tell, as Elizabeth Achtemeier points out. We will want to weave a web of mystery and enchantment—of fairy tale magic, but with the magic being real and the tale being true—around the beings of our listeners, not forgetting to include our own being within it. We will want to invite them to join with us in a joyful dance around the tree of life. And then we will mourn together as the serpent, that symbol of our yearning to twist the dance to our own ends, tempts us, and we fall.

Then together we can relive the birth of new hope, Abraham setting out to found a nation, a nation through which we are blessed today as we worship the God of Abraham, Sarah, Isaac, Jacob, and Ruth. Together we become Jacob, who like us lives his shallow life for his own ends and manipulates all those around him. Then night falls and the night within our hearts rises up to meet it and an enigmatic figure comes to wrestle with us in the dark beside the river. When morning breaks we are wounded, but we are also now Israel, a new being.

The centuries pass, and we walk with Jesus, and his parables explode in our midst, strange and prickly and ungainly things, filling our beings with images we can't understand but can't quite let go—a kingdom like a mustard seed, wise and foolish maidens, rich fools whose souls are demanded of them just when their barns are full at last, religious leaders who pass the mugging victim by.

Jesus calls us to put down our nets and to walk away from our computer terminals, and this is a very hard thing. A few of us reluctantly do it, but Jesus isn't heading where we wanted him to go, he's heading toward Jerusalem, toward a barren windswept hill and death on a cross. So when the cock crows we betray him, three times we betray him.

We are the women, weeping. We are the disciples, downcast, with no alternative but to go back to our nets and our computers and pick up where we left off before that loser fooled us. Then come reports of angels and strange men in white; the tomb is empty; a man walks in a garden, and it is not the gardener; someone eats with us, eats there beside the sea, with us who betrayed him, and he says, "Feed my sheep."

Then he rises into the clouds, our Jesus, and we weep again, but weird winds blow at Pentecost and strange fires flame and we Christians explode from Palestine to spread across the world. We are crucified, we are burned as the

emperors demand that we bow down to them but we shout:
No! we live in a different house of being. The false gods of
the day, the gods of state and mammon, of affluence, of
peace through strength, may clamor for our worship, but we
stand firm. We want to live not in bogus houses of being,
not in great Babylon fallen, but in New Jerusalem. We want
to enter the city and dance again around the tree of life and
cool our feet in the river of life. The son of David, the bright
morning star, the Spirit, the bride, say to the thirsty ones,
"Come!" We are thirsty, and we come.

The House of Being and the War of Myths

If preachers did become convinced that it was their task
to help build such a house of being, why might it be accurate
to describe their undertaking as preaching about social concerns? There are several reasons. One is that the biblical
house of being, an image that overlaps with such terms as
the kingdom of God and the church, is a house into which
all are invited. Its walls are provided to offer justice and
safety and peace, shalom and well-being, to those within,
not to keep out those not yet inside. When the church
moves far enough into its house of being to sense and live
this out, it challenges and sometimes even subverts the
social order, merely (if "merely" is the proper word for an
act that can be so simple yet so radical) by enfolding within
its walls persons whom society normally keeps apart, as
when white and black worship together while racial unrest
flares outside.

Another social implication of building and living in a
biblical house of being arises from the fact that persons who
choose to dwell in it are transformed to the core. They
possess not only a Christian *mind,* as important as that is,
but a Christian *being.* To possess a Christian being is to live
within the multidimensional Christian Story with its majestic mythic fabric; it is to live within what Wilder calls a
"theopoetic" structure. Wilder says that "A theopoetic oriented to today's struggle with the principalities and powers
can overcome their bondage, exorcize their evil, and shape
the human future."[29]

Wilder argues that social action which does not root itself

in this depth dimension—and liberation theology, he charges, is sometimes guilty of this, a charge to which all of us who make social action a priority should probably at times plead guilty—does not ultimately "change men's minds." More effective will be action that operates

> at a deeper level where the wrestling is with the loyalties, banners, and spells that rule a way of life and its institutions. In such an engagement no doubt occasions of public confrontation will arise. When they do Christian action will have a symbolic or dramatic character, enforcing its deeper persuasions. Early Christianity was more like guerilla theater than social revolution, but it overthrew principalities and powers. When Jesus drove out the money changers they were no doubt back again the next day or the next week. But the episode was an acted parable and evoked the powerful theocratic vision of the prophets.[30]

This does not mean Christians should never engage in specific social actions or take specific stands on specific issues. It means there is a more fundamental level of Christian existence than that. Christian existence is like a river, flowing from an underground spring. The river bursts forth from the ground in concrete, visible action, but it would run dry if not fed from below. What took place in biblical days and what takes place today when persons live in a biblical house of being is a war between the Story and the pagan stories that constantly seduce us, pleading with us, like the serpent, to grant them our allegiance. The war is a "war of myths or contest with the idols which goes on in the hidden dramas of the heart" and which "can also come to open conflict in the life of institutions and society."[31]

Among the symbols of the societal myth are credentials, clean bodies, dollars, and sleek cars. The symbols of the Story are a basin and a towel, dusty feet, the Good Samaritan, arms stretched wide to take back a son from feeding the pigs, and a cross reaching up to a sky turned dark at noon.

Those who enter the house of being defined by the second set of symbols will have no choice but to do battle with the structure defined by the first set. Because the societal symbols are apt to be as deeply entrenched in the heart as the Christian ones, the battle will be fiercely fought at the deep levels of being. But if the battle is engaged in (and there will be not one but many) and if victories take place, changed beings will emerge and people will be transformed, marching to a different drummer, hearing that different tune.

People will go up to the mountaintop with Martin Luther King, Jr., and look over and *see* the Promised Land. People will stand with Oscar Romero at the communion rail as he speaks of the bread and wine, Christ's body broken and blood shed to make the world home for all, just before the shots ring out.

People will reject the myth of easy love and self-gratification, stay faithfully married and have children as a sign of their hope in God even as the missiles stand ready in their silos. People will share with other people the good news that in this world, which so often seems barren and devoid of meaning, there *is* a house of being within which all can find shelter, like chicks resting under the tender wing of their mother.

5

Social Justice Preaching:
Some Nuts and Bolts

We have been talking about showing and not merely telling, about the fact that people live not merely by the ideas of their heads but by the "imaginations of the heart," to quote Elizabeth Achtemeier.[1] We have tried at points to do some showing ourselves. We have tried not only to tell about preaching but to show how by weaving into our treatment of various topics sections written in near-sermonic style; sections that could, with some polishing and adaptation to specific settings, actually be preached. We have also, of course, done much telling about what it is that preachers should be showing in their sermons, but we have done it in a relatively general way.

In this chapter we want to focus on telling: we want to discuss some nuts and bolts of preaching, some specific and down-to-earth matters a preacher will have to wrestle with in moving from the kinds of things we have been exploring to preaching actual sermons. This does not mean we will attempt an exhaustive treatment of matters to which whole books have been devoted, such as biblical exegesis and interpretation or sermon construction and delivery. We will, rather, try to interact with just enough of such material to suggest ways it might be linked to the central concerns of this book.

To do that, we will first pick up where we left off in our last chapter: we will look at some of the concrete ways sermons can be constructed to build a house of being that is rooted in the depths. Here we will explore the story form and related matters. Next we will examine the fact that material which emerges from and is more oriented toward the intuition-imagination-feeling side of people does, indeed, need to be tested by critical thought. Then, recognizing that not all the Bible is in narrative form and not all sermons should major in narrative, we will offer brief comment on preaching non-narrative sermons without rejecting a broader narrative framework. Finally, we will examine ways the personality types of preachers and hearers may affect the preaching task.

Preaching in Story Form

As important as the narrative element in preaching is, a sermon in story form need not be swallowed up by story. A sermon does not have to be one extended story, though this will perhaps sometimes be the case, nor do all of its elements need to be narrative ones. Story that is forced to gulp down a sermon whole is likely to treat the sermon the same way the big fish, after three days, treated Jonah. So when we speak of preaching in story form we have in mind preaching that is shaped like a story, communicates as a story does, and that—when it is based on a biblical story—follows in its development the unfolding elements of the story it is expounding.

Such preaching does not simply retell the biblical story but elaborates on it, contemporizes it, connects it to the lives of persons listening thousands of years later. Included within such a treatment can be interludes of "poetry, polemic, anecdote, humor, exegetical analysis, commentary"—though they and the entire sermon will still remain enfolded in a narrative structure that takes a sermon from the stage of once-upon-a-time through then-this-happened to and-this-is-how-it-all-came-out.[2]

Now we want to take a closer look at some of the specific elements or stages a story or story-like sermon might contain. We will be offering pointers, not rules, since story preaching cannot be reduced to rules. And while, for the sake of simplicity, we will speak as if any sermon in story form has discrete stages that unfold in a predictable sequence, some stages may be omitted and the sequence may vary.

We will present just one of many different ways of summarizing the elements of story. Our approach represents a conflation, clarification, and illustration of our own thinking and views held by homileticians like Crum and Lowry, to whom we owe much.[3] It looks like this: Suppose the text to be preached is Luke 10:25–37, which tells the story of the good Samaritan. The preacher's task is to develop a sermon that respects the narrative flow of the text and then connects it to the unfolding stories which are the lives of those listening.

Setting

The first stage in the narrative movement the preacher wants to create might then be exploration of the *setting*, the context, the introduction, the beginning point, the status quo, the equilibrium existing before it is upset. Out of what setting does the good Samaritan story emerge?

The answer is complicated by the fact that there are at least two stories unfolding simultaneously in the same text; there is the story the author of Luke is telling—the story of Jesus—and there is the story Jesus is recorded as telling within the larger account of his own ministry—the story of the Samaritan. This is sometimes the case, that one story unfolds within a larger story. There can be the story told by the text (as when 2 Samuel 12 tells of Nathan and David) and then there can be a story within that story (as when Nathan tells David the story of the rich man and the poor man). There is also another kind of story present in every text, which might be called the "story *behind* the text," having to do with the questions addressed by exegesis. We will say more about that later.

Which layer of story a sermon should primarily address will vary, depending on the preacher's sense of which one is primary in the text, which one will most meaningfully address the situation of the listeners, and which one will allow the sermon to flow in good narrative style.

Suppose in preaching the Samaritan text it is decided that the congregation, like the lawyer who puts Jesus to the test, is asking (though perhaps in a camouflaged form that the preacher will need to uncover), "What shall I do to inherit eternal life?" This can become the setting of the sermon, the beginning point, the context out of which the rest of the sermon will emerge.

Plot

The preacher then incorporates the element of *plot,* of action, of forward movement, into the sermon. He or she introduces a sequence of events or sermonic elements that move the story forward from the setting, its beginning point. In this case that movement will now involve attending to the story-within-a-story of the Samaritan. With the lawyer (who *tests* Jesus), we are struggling with and perhaps rebelling against what it means to have eternal life. Jesus tells us to love God and neighbor. So far so good. Laudable pious principles, those. Equilibrium persists. Then we are asked to listen to a story. Now its plot takes over and moves the sermon onward.

Dynamics

In the next stage the *dynamics* of the story—whether transcendent, structural, personal, or interior—emerge. These have to do with the tissue of relationships, actions, thoughts, feelings, and motivations that help make a story's characters and movement rounded, full-orbed. This is where things get complicated, where the equilibrium is upset. Usually at this point a problem erupts or ambiguity deepens and there is a period of darkness or trouble or uncertainty. In the text, a mugging occurs; a man lies bleeding. Members of Israel's religious ruling class pass him by.

The preacher needs to pull the congregation into these dynamics. How this is done will depend on how the preacher handles a variety of matters, matters that are perhaps most likely to become important in this part of a sermon but that may crop up almost anywhere. They have to do with how one bridges the gap between text and present so that words preserved thousands of years ago can live again, and live in a manner consistent with their original meaning.

There is the matter of *point of view.* The preacher needs to prepare a sermon in such a way that its point of view, its angle of vision, its perspective, is true to the text being preached. Otherwise a sermon will be a bullet ricocheting off the situation it aims to address, as when those who are, in effect, passing by the victims on the Jericho road see themselves as good Samaritans. The text in its current form addresses the point of view of such powerful people as lawyers more than the perspective of the powerless. That point of view will sometimes need to be appropriately translated. A sermon prepared for delivery to persons who are usually at the receiving end of literal and symbolic muggings will approach the text from a different point of view than a sermon prepared for people who have the power to stop muggings or bind up victims.

Once the appropriate point of view has been decided upon, the preacher can offer listeners a bridge between text and present by helping them *identify* with the appropriate characters in a story. In a congregation of the powerless, the preacher might help those listening identify with the man bleeding by the road—or, more fruitfully, might empower them by pointing out that the hero of the story is an outcast such as they. In a congregation of the powerful, the preacher might want to help listeners identify with the powerful ones who pass by. The preacher might want to ask with them why one might pass by, analyzing the situation posed by the story as an aid to entering it.

Another bridge is *analogy*. The preacher has to constantly sort through the data of text and present life to ascertain what in the text is like, or analogous to, persons or situations in the present. Who in the present is like a lawyer or like the Levite with whom Jesus most likely expects the lawyer to identify? A rich American Christian? A denominational leader? Both exegesis and imagination play a part in the establishing of such analogies.

Having established an analogy, a technique that a preacher can use (and have some fun with) to present it is *anachronism*. Anachronism, which was used with great flair and humor by Clarence Jordan in his "Cotton Patch Version" of New Testament books, is the collapsing of the gap between biblical and present time. Instead of stating that this today is *like* that back then, it simply pretends the two are the same and merges them. Here is a passage bristling with anachronism: One day when Jesus was walking down Main Street, a lawyer on his lunch break wandered up to him and asked what he had to do to transcend his existential angst. Jesus told about a man traveling to New York who was mugged at a rest stop on the New Jersey turnpike. . . .

Another way to bridge then and now is through allowing one's immersion in and study of the text to break forth in new *imagery*. The assumption here is that study of the text yields not only ideas but also emotive or intuitive insight. For example, one image a study of the issues of greatness and servanthood visible in Mark 9:33–37 called forth was this contrast: we can try to be important people dwelling in a high, well-fortified castle, or vulnerable children frolicking with other children in the meadow below the castle.[4]

Story. Analogy. Imagery. In one brief acronym (SAI) Edward F. Markquart connects these bridges between text and present, and captures much of what we are concerned to communicate in this section. He makes clear why such bridges are appropriate:

> In his preaching Jesus never said anything without a parable (Matt. 13:34). And so it is today with preachers of the gospel. While in the pulpit . . . we never say anything without using SAIs. Contemporary stories, analogies, and images are the means by which we proclaim the gospel in our preaching. . . . Reason assaults the fortress walls of the mind, but SAIs slip gently through the back door into the heart—and begin to change us.[5]

As we preachers seek to pull hearers gently into the dynamics of the story, it is important, Lowry points out, to involve them not in "contradictories" but in "ambiguities."[6] When we preachers and our hearers pass by the bleeding one it is more likely that we have been caught in ambiguity—several worthy causes asking for our attention—than that we have been offered a choice between two clearly contradictory options, one good and one bad. A sermon which respects that likelihood is more apt to hold attention.

To help our congregations identify, then, with perhaps priest or Levite as a point of entry into the story is not to drag them kicking and screaming into agreement that yes, they *are* in fact calloused boors who could care less about the world's victims. It is instead to wrestle beside them with the pain of what to do when overseas the babies starve and by the road sits a car with hood upraised, but at home waits a tired spouse and two daughters longing for their mommy or their daddy to spend time with them at last.

Climax

So there we all wait, as the story in the text and the stories of our lives unfold within the sermon, wondering how it will finally all turn out, suspense rising. Finally comes the *climax,* that point where all comes to a head, where something has to give, where the gospel is experienced. Here our often-discussed principle of reversal may appear, as the sermon moves toward the climactic moment in which the unexpected erupts. An outcast, a member of that despised group, the Samaritans—or, perhaps, a member of the latest nationality stereotyped as terrorist—passes by, and cares for the wounded man.

What, we will want to wonder in our sermons, might be the climactic moment for us? Might it be, for example, that moment when we sense that those who are the outcasts among us—those poor who don't understand the importance of our VCRs and our BMWs and the jobs that pay enough to buy them—can show us the door into eternal life? Might it be that moment when there breaks into our life the realization that we are tired and lonely and sad in our busy, wealthy lives, and that there just might be other ways we could structure them, ways that would leave us time for our daughters and the broken down cars and the starving babies?

Transformation

Finally comes *transformation,* that moment in the sermon when guidance is given as to ways the insight and energy released at the moment of climax can yield concrete changes. Says Jesus to the lawyer, upon whom it may have just dawned that the outcast Samaritan is guide to eternal life, "Go, and do likewise." And the preacher might want to say to the congregation, though gently and as one caught

in the same bind, "Do you really need all the things that
force you to work at three jobs and leave you with no time
to care? Might there be ways the gospel which has broken
in upon you can transform your priorities and give you new
life?"

Testing the Story

This more intuitive approach to preaching which respects
the narrative and nonrational elements of the Bible and life
needs to be tested. Here rational thought, critical analysis,
logical method come into their own. We stand with Craddock, who says he does not mean by his affirmation of
narrative to "replace rational argument in Christian discourse." He notes:

> Rational argument serves to keep the communication
> self-critical, athletically trim, and free of a sloppy senti-
> mentality that can take over in the absence of critical
> activity. We need always to be warned against the use
> of narratives and stories to avoid the issues of doctrine,
> history and theological reflection.[7]

Rational argument helps the preacher avoid or at least
lessen the ever-present tendency to eisegete, or read truth
into the text, rather than allowing the truth of the text to
transform the reader. This tendency is not lessened, and
perhaps is even heightened, when intuition and imagination
are respected as windows into biblical truth.

Ernest Best is suspicious of some of the very things we
have just finished describing as bridges linking text and
present; he says, for example, that the use of identification
often provides only a false bridge. One reason for this is the
tendency of the person identifying to simply project himself
or herself onto a biblical character, regardless of whether
this is true to the biblical material or not. Another reason
is that identification often creates the illusion that one is
connecting with the biblical situation when in fact the
"situational and cultural embedding of each biblical story"
has been missed.[8] While Best tends to undervalue the nonrational, which leads him sometimes to a too-quick dismissal of the kinds of bridges we have been advocating, his
book also exemplifies the kind of corrective thinking to

which the preacher open to the nonrational should be attentive.

William D. Thompson summarizes specific ways rational judgment helps sermons stay true to the text. He divides the work of wrestling with the biblical text for preaching purposes into two parts, while acknowledging that there is not a neat division between them or full consensus on them in scholarly circles.[9] One part is *exegesis*. It is the task of exegesis to ascertain the meaning of the text in the past, in its original setting, and to wrap boundaries around the meaning it can legitimately be considered to convey in the present.

Thompson sees exegesis as standing on three legs, the "exegetical triad," a triad that in turn stands on the foundation of a reliable version of the text and its accurate translation. There is *literary* exegesis. Form, source, and redaction criticism—which have to do with the literary form and genre of a text, the sources it embodies, and the way a text is shaped by its final editor—are among disciplines that contribute to this area. *Historical* exegesis asks who wrote or edited a text in what place and time, who the intended audience was, and what factors in the cultural, political, religious, or economic background help clarify the meaning of a text. Finally, *theological* exegesis helps us identify and reconstruct the perspectives and assumptions of the biblical writers so that we may have access to the theological intent of a particular body of writing.[10]

The second part of wrestling with the text is *interpretation,* or hermeneutics, whose task is to determine the meaning of the text for the present time. The interpretive task, though indeed a blend of science and art that can never be fully captured by simple rules, does seek to be bound in important ways by the text's original meaning. We have already touched upon some of the material, in our discussion of bridging past and present, which Thompson and others offer in this area.[11]

The Lectionary

We have discussed some of the ways to guard against the idiosyncratic treatment of a particular text. How can one guard against the idiosyncratic *selection* of texts? How is one

Lincoln Christian College

to select the proper portions of the Bible so that they will, together, form a coherent whole? One possibility is for the individual preacher to attempt to understand as fully as possible the outlines of the Story told by the Bible and then break it down into sermon-sized bits and pieces. That process allows the preacher to select those parts of the Story most appropriate for the congregation, but it also inevitably tames the Story, reducing it to whatever dimension the preacher chooses. An important alternative is the use of a lectionary.

The lectionary represents an attempt to select those texts which tell the most important parts of the Story. If, as we have noted earlier, the Bible offers the skeleton of the world's Story, the lectionary offers a skeleton of the biblical Story. The lectionary guides those who follow it through an entire cycle (usually three years) in a retelling of the Story from its beginning to its end.

However, following a lectionary may sometimes make it difficult for a preacher to connect the biblical Story to the congregational story. There will be times when the two can be forced into contact only by stretching one or both out of shape. Suppose homosexuality is the burning issue. The preacher wants to address the issue, but the day's lectionary selection tells of, perhaps, Nathan's judgment of David. Only with marvelous verbal gymnastics can the preacher turn Nathan's and David's interaction into a dialogue on homosexuality.

One possible way of handling this problem, whose feasibility will vary depending on the level of allegiance to the lectionary in the preacher's tradition, would be to follow the lectionary during that period of the church year in which the high points of the Story are retold (roughly Advent through Trinity Sunday), and to deviate from it when necessary during the rest of the year.

There is also a danger of distorting the biblical Story through use of the lectionary. The pairing of Old and New Testament texts can lead one to infer that the Old Testament's only role is to serve as the foil against which the superiority of the New Testament is displayed.[12] The New Testament does complete the Old, but the Old also has truth to offer on its own terms.

Even the very selection of texts, leaving others out, can

be a distortion. The criteria guiding the selection will always be imperfect, sometimes glaringly so, as when a particular text is cut off just before verses affirming reversal. However, a lectionary usually emerges from the confluence of tradition and decisions made by a number of persons working together in its formation. Many more checks and balances thus guide the selection of texts than are present when one preacher chooses texts.

Also, the lectionary is rooted in the Christian year and its centuries of accumulated tradition and ritual, and can remind preachers that the sermon is only part of a totality—part of a worship context that includes not only the spoken word but also music, the Eucharist, and a plethora of nonverbal symbols.

Preaching the Story Without Story

We have suggested that properly prepared sermons will be subjected to critical testing. Among the facts such testing uncovers is that there is, after all, more to the Bible than story. The Story, we insist, provides the framework within which the rest of the Bible develops, so we are not about to back away from the importance of story. But there is no question that within the Story there are all kinds of nonnarrative materials. There is material similar to story, such as poetry, which is filled with imagery, the "I" of SAI. There is also material very unlike story: There are the Levitical codes. Much of Paul's writing, such as his letter to the Romans (a sophisticated theological treatise), unfolds largely through rational argument. There is, along with such undying imagery as lion and lamb together, a large amount of material in the minor and major prophets in the form of direct address.

How do these kinds of material fit into our stress on story? They do so in three ways. First, all texts, even those not in narrative form, do possess a story ingredient. There is, as we mentioned earlier, a story *behind* any text, the story of how the text came to be, the story of the people to whom the text was first addressed, the story of the issues they faced as they tried to live out the Story. A fascinating story lies behind the doctrinal material of Galatians, for example, the story of a people and an apostle struggling, as do Christians still today, with the relationship between gospel and law.

A second way such material fits into our story framework is through a recognition that even non-story material always functions in the context of a larger narrative. Even Leviticus, Paul, Amos, or the driest of dry genealogical lists function—though they are not themselves narrative genres—not so much in isolation from the Story as in clarification of it. Preaching from such material can serve the same clarifying function. Such preaching can tell through direct discourse what it is the Story shows by indirect means.

Third, as we have said elsewhere, there *is* a place for material that tells. There is a place for direct communication. One of the reasons for this, says Craddock, is that the more indirect preaching is, the more it depends on its listeners being solidly rooted in the Story[13]; indirect SAIs (story, analogy, imagery) depend for their power on some contact with the Bible and Christian tradition if they are to convey a preacher's intended meaning. Thus in settings, all too common these days, in which many hearers are poorly grounded in the Bible, there should be sermons that aim to communicate directly.

Direct biblical material can be preached in story form, particularly if the story behind the text provides a central theme, but it is probably better to respect the form of texts that communicate directly and use a direct sermonic form to preach them. One of the best of such forms remains the traditional several-point sermon, what Killinger calls the "developmental" sermon and about which he has kind words to say:

> The reason the classical sermon form—an introduction, two, three, or four points, and a deft conclusion—has endured from the nineteenth century into the present is the same reason it endured from the Middle Ages to the Reformation to the time of Wesley and Whitefield—it is an eminently serviceable way of preparing and communicating a message.[14]

Now even choosing this or other direct forms doesn't negate the use within it of SAIs. The difference is that here they are servants and illustrators of what is told directly. Here there is a concern to put relatively clear boundaries around the meaning being communicated. In indirect preaching, on the other hand, they carry more of the meaning, since in such preaching the intent is not so much to share clearly bounded data as to offer a vessel through which that aspect of the divine which is mysterious can flow.

The entire sermon should, in fact, be bounded by what Thompson calls a central, controlling idea that can be expressed in one sentence.[15] Introduction, points, conclusion, and SAIs are all controlled by that one central idea. The preacher preaching this type of sermon knows where it is going and why. Propositional clarity is deliberately chosen as a balance to the equally deliberate imprecision used at other times to foster transparency to the transcendent.

The Direct Form and Personality Differences

We have been arguing that preaching which tells is valid when it reflects the form of the biblical text (our assumption being that the form of the text is an important clue to the appropriate sermonic form). We have also suggested that showing will not work for persons lacking sufficient grounding in the Story to grasp the nuances of an indirect approach. At this point we want to note another reason for including telling-based sermons in the preaching repertoire: people take in life's data and process their life experience in different ways. Some will like story; many are starved for it. Others will respond coolly to story. They prefer ideas; idea-centered preaching is what will best reach them, and their needs must be respected.

Morton T. Kelsey, using Jung's work, suggests that each of us tends toward a different personality type and that our lives, our theology, our walk of faith, our preaching preferences are colored by it. He identifies first of all a broad division between extroversion and introversion. Extroverts are oriented toward the outer world, toward external forces, toward involvement with many people. They tend to be energized by such involvement. Social action might attract them. Introverts are excited by their inner world. They are often bookworms and dreamers. Too much involvement with the external world drains them, so they crave time alone to recharge. They would tend to be the Christian contemplatives.

People also tend to fit into types according to whether they are interested in concrete things, which might be true of a building contractor; whether they like lofty, abstract thinking, which might characterize two people arguing the merits of existentialism versus logical positivism while their spouses pointedly ignore them; whether they value images and intuitions and nonrational insights, which might be true of an artist; or whether they value human feeling and experience as guides to living, which might be true of a counselor. Kelsey, following Jung, summarizes the types as sensing, thinking, intuiting, and feeling.[16]

People are more complex than such stereotypical generalization can imply, and such typing is controversial. But the fact remains that, however one interprets the phenomena, people display different styles in their approach to life and its data. An example of how this works itself out on the homiletical scene can be found through contrasting the styles of John R. W. Stott and Frederick Buechner.[17]

Stott's book on preaching, *Between Two Worlds,* is a thorough, admirable work, one that is consistent with and lays the groundwork for the kind of preaching that is Stott's strength—preaching that takes the bone of a biblical text and relentlessly gnaws on it until no meat is left and perhaps the marrow itself has been partially digested. Such preaching springs from, and will likely communicate powerfully with, a sharp intellect, one skilled in using logic and clear propositions to communicate truth. An encounter with Stott leaves one experiencing the exhilaration of a freshly sharpened mind. Yet Stott may strike the more intuitive person as a trifle dry.

In contrast, look at Buechner's *Telling the Truth.* To enter Buechner's world is to enter a world of wonder and magic, of intuitions and dreams, of intimations of things that lie just below the surface or around the corner. Buechner is a dreamer who will thrill dreamers; he may sometimes strike the rationalist as a fuzzy-headed mystic (which is not to disparage his intellect).

Much preaching, particularly social justice preaching, uses Stott's approach, with its relatively traditional, telling-based elements (though we are simply noting a general trend in Stott, not suggesting he never values or uses showing-based methods). Believing that the telling-based type of preaching is well covered elsewhere, we have chosen to focus on a preaching style not as often associated with social justice preaching, and to note some of the potential deficiencies of preaching which mainly tells.

Yet our approach should ultimately complement, not fully replace, other methods. That is because all truth, logical or intuitive, is God's truth, and because different preachers and different congregations will, at different times, profit from different styles of communication. Not all preachers will be best suited to story preaching—nor will all do propositional preaching well. And not all listeners will benefit from the same style.

An example of integration of styles is offered by C. S. Lewis, of whom it has been said that he possessed a "feeling intellect." In his nonfiction works, Lewis displays the razor of intellect; in his fiction works (such as his science fiction space trilogy or the Narnia books), he opens the door to worlds of enchantment.

The preacher who respects the implications of differing personal styles will take into account his or her own style with its gifts and deficiencies, evaluate congregational needs, ponder the strengths and weaknesses of different preaching styles, and gradually arrive at the right mix of approaches for a particular context.

6

From Ivory Tower
to Life in the Story

Up to this point we have assumed that we all sit together cozily, authors and readers pondering together in our studies and our ivory towers this strange and wonderful topic of preaching about matters of national and international import. Now it is time to move out into the congregation, into the pulpit with sermon in hand or mind, and to look into the faces and hearts and lives of those who sit before us, waiting with their myriad of hopes and expectations and boredoms and cynicisms for the sermon to begin. It is time to travel from the study to real life. Once the concerns we have been addressing have been worked into actual sermons, what elements exposed by contact with the congregation remain to be considered?

Two primary elements call for our attention. The relationship between us preachers and our congregations is one. The other is the relationship between the Bible, and the God revealed in it, and a congregation—do God and the Bible judge or comfort? Do they support the status quo or call for new obedience?

Preachers as Fellow Pilgrims

We authors are ultimately not so much the experts telling those reading this book what they need to do to become perfect preachers, as we are fellow pilgrims, groping with our readers toward a destination we will reach, if at all, only after a lifetime of preaching. That same truth, that they are fellow pilgrims with their congregants, needs to lie at the heart of all preachers' relationships with their congregations. Social justice preaching tempts the preacher to speak as if the Lord of Hosts stands in the pulpit and speaks the truth and nothing but the truth. This, the preacher thunders, is what is going on in Central America, and this is what you should think about it, and this is what you should do about it, and—by the way—that's exactly what God thinks you should do, too, as any intelligent reading of the scriptures makes clear!

Preachers who understand that they are not God, after all, but rather puny humans; that they are truly fellow seekers with their congregants—such preachers are the ones who will earn an audience. They will be heard not as savage prophets flailing the unfaithful, but as tender shepherds who care for the lost sheep because they themselves have been, and are sometimes still, lost.

There are several ways a preacher can make clear this status as fellow pilgrim. One is to provide a mechanism— perhaps a sermon-preparation group or a Sunday school class devoted to interaction with sermons—that allows the sermon to grow out of congregational life and not just out of the pastor's study.

Another is through the judicious use of *autobiography* in sermons. Frederick Buechner says:

> At its heart most theology, like most fiction, is essentially autobiography. Aquinas, Calvin, Barth, Tillich, working out their own systems in their own ways and in their own language, are all telling us the stories of their lives, and if you press them far enough, even at their most cerebral and forbidding, you find an experience of flesh and blood, a human face smiling or frowning or weeping or covering its eyes before something that happened once.[1]

When we preachers tell what happened once in our lives, what personal struggle lies behind what we are preaching, we cease to be cerebral or forbidding. This is not to say it is appropriate to share just anything that happened once or is happening now, or that autobiography should become a cloying and wearying component of every sermon. The preaching norms of bygone days and of some circles today, which rejected autobiographical preaching as too self-centered or subjective or improper, were perhaps too prim, too colored by a rationalism that didn't understand that theology *is*, to a significant extent, autobiography. But they held some truth; the point of preaching is not to impose the preacher's idiosyncratic view of life on helpless listeners. The point of autobiographical sharing is to locate the preacher in the midst of the congregation as fellow pilgrim, not to spew forth matters only spouses or therapists or God should be forced to hear.

The Preacher/Congregation Relationship with the Bible and God

One reason it is crucial for the preacher to be a fellow pilgrim is that to preach is to share good news, it is to tell the wondrous Story. But the goodness of the news is experienced in a variety of ways: sometimes as empowering grace, sometimes as accepting and comforting grace—but sometimes as a savage grace.

Savage Grace

God who loves all, not only rich and powerful but also poor and weak and outcast, is sometimes experienced as savage by those who have to be burned before they can be healed. Thus, we write of a savage grace.

If it is indeed the case (though we acknowledge that this is open to debate) that the rich industrialized nations of the West bear some responsibility for the hunger and poverty afflicting much of the rest of the world; if nuclear weapons, which exist partly to defend such wealth, are immoral; if the destruction of rain forests and the stockpiling of nuclear and toxic wastes is a desecration of God's good earth; if favoring self-fulfillment over commitment is wrong—then to preach appropriately to those implicated in such immorality, through membership in societies that perpetuate it, is to do more than simply offer balm from Gilead.

Now, to preach to those who are *oppressed* by the structural evil of the world *is* to offer balm, and to share the empowerment of the Jesus who liberates captives. But we have been assuming that preachers who read this book are more apt to be preaching to those in powerful societies than those in oppressed societies. So we want to focus here on how one preaches about social issues to those who have some power.

To preach in such a context *is* at times to offer not balm but savage grace. It is to proclaim that there is a Story waiting to be lived out, but some hard choices will have to be made by those who want to enter into it. It is to remind people that when God breaks in and Jesus comes, life does not go on as usual but gets turned upside down, and fishing nets lie unused and drying by the sea.

Such preaching does not mean repeatedly hitting people with hard words of judgment. It should usually mean, once again, traveling with one's congregants, sharing with them the growing understanding that what those in the affluent West often think is good news is actually bad news; that it is oppressive, and not liberating, to watch television commercials celebrating the good life while one sits behind computerized triple-security burglar alarms blinking their red electronic eyes. The aim is finally not to convince people that they are bad but to help them explore the possibility that there is a good news far better than the good news the world loves.

In Luke 12:49–51 one finds these troubling words: "I came to cast fire upon the earth; and would that it were already kindled! . . . Do you think that I have come to give peace on earth? No . . ." What is this fiery Jesus doing in the same gospel that records such tender stories as those of the prodigal son and the good Samaritan? What do such words mean? Might it be they warn that when an age or a society or a world is sick the healing can hurt?

In *The Manticore*, a novel by Robertson Davies, Staunton is undergoing Jungian analysis. As he struggles to understand and come to terms with the various components of his psyche, he remembers and dreams about Felix, a toy bear he played with as a child, a bear who was a friend when life turned rough. His analyst suggests that Felix symbolizes that part of him which will befriend him, which will nurture him and comfort him on his journey toward wholeness. But, she warns, "even the Friend is not always benevolent; sometimes friends are truest when they seem unfriendly." And she implies that the fact that Felix is a bear may serve as a similar warning—a friend symbolized by a savage animal is apt to offer friendship tinged with savagery.[2]

C. S. Lewis makes an analogous point from a Christian perspective in *The Lion, the Witch, and the Wardrobe,* one of his Narnia books for children. Aslan, the majestic lion who functions as Christ-figure in the land of Narnia, is comforter, guide, savior to those who love him, but he is not a tame lion, as anyone who tangles with him comes to understand. He is a *good* lion, yes, but his goodness is a terrible goodness, and sometimes salvation is bought at the price of lion claws raked across one's back.

One day Aslan dies, offering his life in place of one who has been captured by the dread White Witch. He is killed by animals who mock him and shear off his fur and leave him looking small and ugly. His death appears to be a victory for the dark spirit of the age; it appears, even to those who love him, to be bad news, because they are creatures of their age, and, according to their understanding of life, death—especially such an ignominious death as this one—is defeat.

But none of them—neither those who hate Aslan and glory in their triumph, nor those who love him and weep by his dead and shorn lion's body—know of the Deep Magic from Before the Dawn of Time and its effect on a victim willing to die for another. The Deep Magic rumbles forth and cracks open the brittle shell of the old age, and Aslan, beloved great lion Aslan, lives and roars again. The world's good news turns out to be bad news, and the bad news turns out to be goodness such as makes hair stand straight up.[3]

Empowering Grace

If this word of savage grace is heard, and preacher and congregation together allow God to transform their lives, then another kind of grace will begin to emerge. This is the good news that the God who—through the words of scripture, the example and teachings of Jesus, and the promptings of the Holy Spirit—calls for change also offers power to change.

The early Anabaptist tradition of the 1500s suggests an understanding of grace as *empowerment.* In Protestantism, says Robert Friedmann, there has been "an overstressed view of grace . . . understood as the marvelous force which alone redeems the sinner in spite of all his shortcomings."[4]

Friedmann suggests that while this understanding of grace as justification was not entirely foreign to early Anabaptism, and while Anabaptist theology tended to be more a lived theology than a systematic theology (so that one should not press subtle distinctions too hard), grace in Anabaptism meant more than forgiveness: "Grace . . . meant the inner power to resist sin." Grace granted to the Christian the Holy Spirit's power, "the 'inner light' which enabled the believer to walk the path of righteousness and to visualize the cross as the likely consequence, interpreting suffering as a step to greater blessedness."[5]

God's grace was thus understood as empowering gift, as God's presence giving the follower of Jesus the courage to continue following even unto death. This empowering grace allowed the early Anabaptists to survive persecution and to stand to this day as an example of a people remaining doggedly true to their faith. Yet this empowering grace was not, of course, the possession solely of the Anabaptists. Augustine, Aquinas, Wesley, Barth, and more—not to mention the apostle Paul—knew of such grace. And it is evident all around the world today, wherever Christians refuse to bow to Caesar, no matter what the cost.

Their understanding of grace led Anabaptists toward a type of biblical interpretation Ben C. Ollenburger calls "the hermeneutics of obedience." He says, "The Anabaptist genius lay not in any exegetical technique or hermeneutical novelty or even in any theological discoveries, but rather in the simple (and expensive) commitment to do what Jesus says." The implication of this for present study of the Bible, says Ollenburger, is that "we must read the Bible as regenerated, obedient people, followers of Christ first and foremost."[6]

Liberation theology has similar things to say. It argues, basically, that one cannot fully understand the Bible from a purely theoretical and objective stance; one must instead enter into the world the Bible delineates if one is to understand it. "Correct knowledge is contingent on right doing. Or rather, the knowledge is disclosed in the doing," says José Míguez-Bonino.[7]

James H. Cone, wrestling with the insights of Marx and Feuerbach and the sociology of knowledge, comes to the conclusion that our social setting produces within each of us an "axiological grid" or a particular set of spectacles through which we view reality. He further argues that some lenses allow more accurate perception of the Bible than do others. Eyes peering through the lenses of spectacles ground by such oppression and poverty and slavery as black people have undergone are more likely to perceive clearly the meaning of the exodus than are eyes peering through lenses never subjected to such refinement. Thus some social contexts aid clear reading of the Bible; others distort it.[8]

To preach empowering grace is to share the good news that, in the midst of the painful changes God calls us to consider, God's enabling presence throbs. It means for preacher and congregation to realize that the more they follow Jesus, the more they will understand what it means to follow Jesus. The farther into the biblical house of being they choose to go, the better they will understand what its walls are made of. The more concretely they choose to live out the Story, the better they will understand where the Story is going. The preacher's task is to serve as the catalyst starting such cycles of obedience leading to further knowledge, in turn leading to deeper obedience.

Comforting Grace

After all the disquieting things we have said about savage and empowering grace, there is, however, still that notion of justifying grace, that sometimes overstressed yet certainly important notion of grace as "the marvelous force which alone redeems the sinner in spite of all his shortcomings." Grace understood in this mode is grace that unconditionally accepts, that lays tender hands upon the wounded soul. When repentant, even those most implicated in Western affluence, worship of arms, or destruction of the earth can experience the radical forgiveness offered through Jesus.

This assurance also must be voiced by the preacher wrestling with the large issues of the day. There is a time to talk of savage grace and a time to talk of empowering grace. But there is also a time to recognize that as necessary as change is if our world is to survive its woes, as much as we need sometimes to face our complicity in such woes, we are also all sad and fearful and broken human beings who feel overwhelmed by the world's troubles. We know change is needed and we know we are called to play a part, but we aren't sure what it is and we need to hear that the yoke Jesus gives to us is easy and his burden is light.

How, beyond the crucial first step of highlighting the forgiveness Jesus offers, does the preacher offer that comfort? One way is through remembering to understand and preach social issues in all their *multidimensional* complexity. When this is done the preacher can help congregants understand that while all are called to some involvement in the world's pain, all are also called according to their gifts and abilities and energies. Some may be called to help governments respond more effectively to pain at the structural level; some to risk their lives through service in Central America; others to love their neighbor, in particular their friends with the handicapped baby they courageously chose not to abort; still others to intercede in prayer, in the quiet of the night under the cozy bedcovers.

Another way the preacher comforts is through acknowledging that while in relation to some of the world's pressing issues we in the rich nations may prove to be as much villains as heroes and heroines in God's Story, most of us are also wounded and afflicted and torn. Though we are members of societies that sometimes victimize others, we are also often victims ourselves, of abusive spouses or parents, of tragic accidents, of crippled minds and emotions and spirits and bodies. God, we believe, cares about such victimization as well. God promises that those who so hurt now will someday leap with joy.

A third (and related) way to comfort is to make clear in our preaching that while God's Story *is* rife with reversal, it is also filled with comfort, with the assurance that down below the level of God's surprises there sturdily stands the bedrock of God's love. Craddock warns against "preaching surprises Sunday after Sunday to flocks no longer surprised. No church can thrive on a strict diet of O. Henry. [The] wise course to follow is to keep direct and indirect, normalcy and reversal, justice and grace, both present in the content and style of our communicating."[9]

There *is* a time to surprise, affirms Craddock, but there is also a time to remember that "all listeners at times need no surprises."[10] There is a time to remember that lapping within each listener, as well as in the preacher, are those

oceans of suppressed feeling, that psychic numbing produced by living in a world filled with trouble and tears. At
such times the preacher is called to listen to the signals of
distress, to hear the pleas of the drowning, to throw out a
lifeline and pull the shivering soul into a dry and warm place.

In many congregations, the proper entry point into
preaching about national and international concerns may
well be the recognition that people cannot bear to hear
about the judgment of God's love and the power of God's
love until they sense that the one addressing them feels
their pain. But if we preachers can touch our own pain
honestly enough to empathize with our hearers' pain, and
if we can demonstrate to them that we share their tears and
are moved to compassion by them, the door into the Story
may begin to open. Step by step and year by year we may
together find ourselves moving farther and farther into the
Story with no end.

Buechner tells of a dream he had one night:

> I am sitting on a stool at a bar, and my glass has left a
> wet ring on the wooden counter-top. With my finger,
> I start to move the wet around. I move it this way and
> that way with nothing much on my dream of a mind.
> And then on the smooth counter of the bar I write a
> name. When I have finished writing it, I start to weep,
> and the tears wake me up. I cannot remember the name
> I wrote, but I know that it was a name I was willing to
> die for. Maybe it was the secret name of God or the
> secret name of the world. Maybe it was my own secret
> name. The dream is only a dream, but the tears are
> exceedingly real.[11]

Maybe through our preaching, and our joint pilgrimage
with those to whom we preach, we can, over the days and
years, enter the land of dreams which is the Story. Maybe
we can journey into that land filled with the intimation that
the Story offers a dream that doesn't just quiver inside us
at night but turns solid and real with the coming of day.
Maybe as we travel the paths of that land we will remember
the name for which we weep. Maybe we will at last realize
that each of our names is the name of a character living out
a Story told by the one whose Name is beyond all names,
and that to be thus named is beautiful.

Appendix:
Finding Information on the Issues

There are four basic resources the preacher can turn to in the quest for a modicum of expertise: educational, organizational, experiential, and printed resources. The print resources are listed separately, in the Bibliography. In addition, while we will not offer a detailed guide to them, there are many audiovisual resources.

Educational Resources

Most preachers need a reasonable amount of formal training to function competently in a role that demands some understanding of a complex world. As preachers undertake that training, they can be alert to courses and field placements that deepen their understanding of social issues. Once a preacher has finished a particular phase of formal training, it is time to take advantage of the continuing-education options offered by many colleges and seminaries; here, too, options focusing on social issues can be chosen.

The preacher can also be on the lookout for seminars and conferences with appropriate themes, such as those that focus on specific issues, on preaching about social issues or, perhaps, on the integration of spirituality and a concern for social justice. *Sojourners* and *The Other Side* are among magazines that regularly offer updates on relevant conferences and retreats.

Organizational Resources

There are numerous organizations devoted to analyzing or interacting with particular issues. Generally such an organization will make regular mailings of literature to inform interested persons of the latest thinking and events in whatever domain the organization considers its own. The vision, ideology, and integrity of such organizations vary widely, but a preacher who, after inspection, joins several is likely to find that such membership provides valuable links to a larger group's expertise and energy.

Among examples of organizations devoted to interaction with some of the issues we explored in chapter 3 are: Evangelicals for Social Action (which attempts to keep members abreast of current issues such as peace, justice, liberty, and the sanctity of life); the American Friends Service Committee (which promotes peace and justice around the world); and Habitat for Humanity (which provides housing for the poor); also World Vision, Church World Service, and the Mennonite Central Committee (which work at relief and development around the world). *The Other Side* (March 1985, pp. 36–47) has published a list of thirty-five such organizations, describing their purpose and how they use money given to them. Also, most denominations have offices that disseminate information about issues.

Experiential Resources

Another way a preacher can gain insight into social issues is through personal immersion in them. The way in which the preacher becomes involved in an issue will vary, but a multidimensional understanding of the issues can at least provide a general guide to possible options.

Preachers can gain significant access to the *interior* dimension of many issues by looking within themselves, by gaining some understanding of how their own depths are affected by particular issues. They will often gain access to the *personal* dimension of issues simply through their work as faithful pastors with those in their congregations affected by an issue, such as unemployment. The preacher can also choose to identify with and relate to a group in the community, such as the homeless. In such a situation the preacher will be face to face with the interior and personal dimensions of the issues, but will also want to explore the larger *structural* matters that have helped bring about the suffering of particular people. She or he may also be forced to break through the despair that such involvement can provoke into contact with the *transcendent* dimension, into faith that bleak realities are not necessarily final realities.

One experiential resource a preacher could consider, perhaps for a sabbatical, would be to spend time working with a volunteer organization. Many Protestant denominations and Catholic groups sponsor voluntary service organizations. Because many of them work with people torn by social forces, involvement with them could give a volunteering preacher important insight. *The Other Side* (January–February 1986, pp. 21–28) has published a guide to twenty-nine voluntary service organizations.

An option that will not be feasible for everyone, and that can degenerate into the paradox of luxurious junkets organized to understand the poor, is to travel to places particularly affected by certain issues. A preacher may benefit for a lifetime from a sensitively undertaken venture to Central America, torn as it is by poverty and injustice and war. Such a venture could help graphically to clarify the multidimensional impact of such factors as corporate exploitation or government by the rich and for the rich.

In addition to his or her own experience, the preacher can draw upon the experience of others within the congregation. Not only can the preacher obtain information from persons with expertise in specific occupational and vocational fields, but also the very act of turning to such people may involve them in dealing with the issue at hand. As this begins to happen, a potent cycle can be set up in which the preacher catalyzes thinking and action on an issue, which can create feedback helping to test and refine the preacher's own ideas and conceptualizations, which in turn can stimulate further thought and action, and so on. What results is a community of people mobilized to bring their combined resources to bear on social issues. No longer, then, will one or two inevitably limited leader/preachers try vainly to move intractable mountains. Instead, all can live out their adventure Story together; together they can generate the faith that will move the mountains.

Notes

Chapter 1: Peace, Justice, and Fairy Tales

1. Alfred Krass, "The Limits of Words," *The Other Side*, July 1985, p. 70.

2. Ibid.

3. José Miranda, *Marx and the Bible: A Critique of the Philosophy of Oppression* (Maryknoll, N.Y.: Orbis Books, 1974), p. 44.

4. Ibid., p. 48.

5. Stanley Hauerwas and William H. Willimon, "Embarrassed by God's Presence," *The Christian Century*, January 30, 1985, pp. 98–100.

6. Mircea Eliade, *The Sacred and the Profane: The Nature of Religion* (New York: Harcourt, Brace & Co., 1959), p. 203.

7. Hauerwas and Willimon, "Embarrassed by God's Presence," p. 100.

8. A. James Reimer, "The Nature and Possibility of a Mennonite Theology," *The Conrad Grebel Review* (Winter 1983), p. 44, note 37.

9. Eliade, *The Sacred and the Profane*, p. 202.

10. Michael A. King, "Their Haunting Secret," *Christian Living*, April 1985, p. 18.

11. Richard A. Jensen, *Telling the Story: Variety and Imagination in Preaching* (Minneapolis: Augsburg Publishing House, 1980), pp. 28–41.

12. Eugene L. Lowry, *Doing Time in the Pulpit: The Relationship Between Narrative and Preaching* (Nashville: Abingdon Press, 1985), pp. 14–17.

13. Ibid., p. 15.

14. Elizabeth Achtemeier, *Creative Preaching: Finding the Words* (Nashville: Abingdon Press, 1980), p. 44.

15. Gabriel Fackre, *The Christian Story: A Narrative Interpretation of Basic Christian Doctrine* (Grand Rapids: Wm. B. Eerdmans Publishing Co., 1978), p. 83.

16. Ibid.

17. Ibid., p. 98.

18. Ibid., pp. 111–126.

19. J. R. R. Tolkien, "On Fairy-Stories," in *Essays Presented to Charles Williams*, ed. by C. S. Lewis (Grand Rapids: Wm. B. Eerdmans Publishing Co., 1966), p. 81.

20. Ibid., p. 84.

21. Frederick Buechner, *Telling the Truth: The Gospel as Tragedy, Comedy, and Fairy Tale* (San Francisco: Harper & Row, 1977), pp. 95–96.

22. Ibid., pp. 96–97.

23. Ibid., p. 97. Just in case Buechner refers here to reincarnation, let it be clear that is not something we would affirm.

Chapter 2: Story and the Dimensions of the Issues

1. Ed Magnuson, "Fixing NASA," *Time*, June 9, 1986, pp. 14–25.

2. Eugene L. Lowry, *Doing Time in the Pulpit* (Nashville: Abingdon Press, 1985), p. 44.

3. Ibid.

4. Ibid.

5. Leo N. Tolstoy, *War and Peace*, tr. by Rosemary Edmonds (Harmondsworth, Middlesex, England: Penguin Books, 1957).

6. John Howard Yoder, *The Politics of Jesus* (Grand Rapids: Wm. B. Eerdmans Publishing Co., 1972), p. 139.

7. G. B. Caird, *Principalities and Powers: A Study in Pauline Theology* (London: Oxford University Press, 1956), p. vii. Among Pauline references one might cite are Eph. 3:10; Col. 2:8, 15; 3:20; Gal. 4:3, and many more.

8. Yoder, *The Politics of Jesus*, p. 139, note 2. Yoder is commenting on Berkhof's thought (see our note 10, below).

9. Gustaf Aulén, *Interpretation*, Jan. 1951, pp. 156–158, quoted in F. W. Dillistone, *The Christian Understanding of Atonement* (Philadelphia: Westminster Press, 1968), pp. 104–105. The *Christus Victor* theory of the atonement is the focus of our discussion only because it clarifies the relationship between structural evil and Christ's work on the cross, not because it provides the only valid understanding. Other theories would come into focus if our discussion centered elsewhere—such as on the forgiveness of personal sin.

10. Hendrik Berkhof, *Christ and the Powers*, tr. by John Howard Yoder (Scottdale, Pa.: Herald Press, 1962), p. 22.

11. Yoder, *The Politics of Jesus*, pp. 145–146.

12. Ibid., p. 143.

13. Jim Wallis, *Agenda for Biblical People* (New York: Harper & Row, 1976), p. 63.

14. Yoder, *The Politics of Jesus*, p. 132.

15. Ibid., p. 133.

16. Ibid., p. 162.

17. John Sanford, *The Kingdom Within: A Study of the Inner Meaning of Jesus' Sayings* (Philadelphia: J. B. Lippincott Co., 1970), pp. 111–112. Sanford's approach risks a psychologization, and a consequent reduction of the Story's interior dimension akin to the flattening we have suggested is risked by those committed to the structural perspective. While in this section we use the views of Sanford and others as examples of how one might translate the Story into terms amenable to modern, psychologically oriented perspectives, we do not mean to suggest that the Christian Story should be viewed only from such angles.

18. Ibid., p. 138.

19. Don S. Browning, *Atonement and Psychotherapy* (Philadelphia: Westminster Press, 1966), pp. 182, 247.

20. F. W. Dillistone, *The Christian Understanding of Atonement*, p. 113.

21. Charles Williams, *Descent Into Hell* (1937; Grand Rapids: Wm. B. Eerdmans Publishing Co., 1979), pp. 124–125.

22. Garrison Keillor, "Letter from Jim," *News from Lake Wobegon: Original Monologues; Spring* (Minnesota Public Radio, 1983; cassette tape).

23. Jim Wallis, *Agenda for Biblical People*, pp. 100, 128.

Chapter 3: The Biblical Story's Perspective on Key Issues

1. Frederick Buechner, *Telling the Truth: The Gospel as Tragedy, Comedy, and Fairy Tale* (San Francisco: Harper & Row, 1977), p. 79.

2. Eugene L. Lowry, *Doing Time in the Pulpit* (Nashville: Abingdon Press, 1985), p. 57.

3. Eugene L. Lowry, *The Homiletical Plot: The Sermon as Narrative Art Form* (Atlanta: John Knox Press, 1980), p. 48.

4. Lowry, *Doing Time in the Pulpit*, p. 57.

5. Ronald J. Sider, *Rich Christians in an Age of Hunger: A Biblical Study*, 2nd ed. (Downers Grove, Ill.: Inter-Varsity Press, 1984), p. 54.

6. Ibid., pp. 54–61. See this section for a fuller treatment of these three crucial moments of divine intervention.

7. Buechner, *Telling the Truth*, p. 89.

8. Ibid., p. 90.

9. Ibid.

10. Justo L. Gonzalez and Catherine G. Gonzalez, *Liberation Preaching: The Pulpit and the Oppressed* (Nashville: Abingdon Press, 1980), p. 19.

11. Ibid., pp. 52–53. See also Sider, *Rich Christians in an Age of Hunger,* pp. 75–76.

12. The Bible often uses words for the fetus that are applied normally to persons already born—Gen. 25:22; 38:27ff.; Job 1:21; 3:3, 11ff.; 10:18ff.; 31:15; Isa. 44:2, 24; 49:5; Jer. 20:14–18; Hosea 12:3. Passages that assume continuity between the fetus and the child after birth include Jer. 1:5; Pss. 51:5; 139:13–16. A study by the Orthodox Presbyterian Church suggests, on the other hand, that one cannot prove, based on scripture or science, that the unborn child is unquestionably a person from the point of conception ("Report of the Committee to Study the Matter of Abortion," in *Minutes of the Thirty-eighth General Assembly,* May 24–29, 1971, p. 146; The Orthodox Presbyterian Church, 7401 Old York Road, Philadelphia, PA 19126).

13. For exposure of the argument that the cost of caring for handicapped children justifies abortion, see Norman B. Bendroth, "Abortion and the Third Way of the Kingdom," in Richard Cizik, ed., *The High Cost of Indifference* (Ventura, Calif.: Regal Books, 1983), p. 58.

14. Ethel Waters, with Charles Samuels, *His Eye Is on the Sparrow: An Autobiography* (Garden City, N.Y.: Doubleday & Co., 1951), pp. 3–4.

15. *Scientific American,* June 1980, p. 42.

16. Philip G. Ney, "A Consideration of Abortion Survivors," *Child Psychiatry and Human Development,* vol. 13, no. 3 (Spring 1983), p. 170.

17. Richard Batey, *Jesus and the Poor* (New York: Harper & Row, 1972), p. 92.

18. Gonzalez, *Liberation Preaching,* pp. 77–78.

19. Rubem Alves, *I Believe in the Resurrection of the Body,* tr. by L. M. McCoy (Philadelphia: Fortress Press, 1986), p. 57.

20. We are not here affirming poverty or asceticism as Christian virtues; the earth and its abundance are good. But, for the sake of our mission in the world, we—as followers of the incarnate Jesus—need to identify with the poor and marginalized. See Sider, *Rich Christians in an Age of Hunger,* especially pp. 163–190, for a fuller guide to downward mobility and simple living.

21. Rosemary Radford Ruether, "Feminism and Peace," *The Christian Century,* Aug. 31–Sept. 7, 1983, p. 775.

22. Ibid.

23. Ibid. Ruether's vision includes components that are sometimes affirmed by "New Age" thinkers. See Ronald J. Sider,

"Green Politics: Biblical or Buddhist?" *Spiritual Counterfeits Project Newsletter,* Fall 1985, pp. 7–11, for comment on the distinction between our approach and the New Age perspective.

24. See H. Paul Santmire, "The Liberation of Nature: Lynn White's Challenge Anew," *The Christian Century,* May 22, 1985, pp. 530–533, for a discussion of Lynn White's thesis that Christianity has much to answer for in relation to ecological problems.

25. Thomas Merton, *Contemplative Prayer* (New York: Herder & Herder, 1969), pp. 27–28.

26. Thomas Merton, ed., *Gandhi on Nonviolence* (New York: New Directions, 1965), p. 6.

27. See Ronald J. Sider and Richard K. Taylor, *Nuclear Holocaust and Christian Hope: A Book for Christian Peacemakers* (Downers Grove, Ill.: Inter-Varsity Press, 1982), pp. 121–134 (and the literature cited) for a fuller treatment of Jesus' nonviolent way.

Chapter 4: Building a Biblical House of Being

1. John R. W. Stott, *Between Two Worlds: The Art of Preaching in the Twentieth Century* (Grand Rapids: Wm. B. Eerdmans Publishing Co., 1982), p. 170.

2. Amos Wilder, *Early Christian Rhetoric: The Language of the Gospel* (London: SCM Press, 1964), p. 64.

3. Ibid., pp. 64–65.

4. Elizabeth Achtemeier, *Creative Preaching: Finding the Words* (Nashville: Abingdon Press, 1980), p. 45.

5. Amos Wilder, *Jesus' Parables and the War of Myths: Essays on Imagination in the Scriptures,* ed. by James Breech (Philadelphia: Fortress Press, 1982), p. 54.

6. Ibid.

7. Amos Wilder, *Theopoetic: Theology and the Religious Imagination* (Philadelphia: Fortress Press, 1976), p. 75.

8. Wilder, *Early Christian Rhetoric,* p. 128.

9. Stott, *Between Two Worlds,* p. 170.

10. Wilder, *Jesus' Parables and the War of Myths,* pp. 51–52.

11. Ibid., p. 51.

12. Ibid., p. 55.

13. David Tracy, *The Analogical Imagination: Christian Theology and the Culture of Pluralism* (Crossroad Publishing Co., 1981), cited in Calvin R. Mercer, "Norman Perrin's Pilgrimage: Releasing the Bible to the Public," *The Christian Century,* May 14, 1986, p. 485.

14. See Ronald J. Sider, "Green Politics: Biblical or Buddhist?" *Spiritual Counterfeits Project Newsletter,* Fall 1985, pp. 7–11, for a clarification of where the line falls between our thinking and "New Age" thinking—which deserves some criticism.

15. Fred B. Craddock, *Overhearing the Gospel* (Nashville: Abingdon Press, 1978), p. 133.

16. Walter Wink, *Transforming Bible Study* (Nashville: Abingdon Press, 1980), pp. 21–26.

17. Ibid., pp. 31–32. We do not mean to suggest that the collective unconscious equals God. We reject philosophical monism and pantheism and affirm a clear distinction between Creator and creature. Again, see "Green Politics," note 14, above.

18. June Singer, *Boundaries of the Soul: The Practice of Jung's Psychology* (Garden City, N.Y.: Doubleday & Co., Anchor Books, 1973), pp. 85–88.

19. Ibid., pp. 89–90.

20. Ibid., pp. 94–96.

21. Carl G. Jung, *The Collected Works of Carl G. Jung*, tr. by R. F. C. Hull, vol. IX, part I (Princeton: Princeton University Press, 1969), p. 79.

22. Ibid., p. 79; Singer, *Boundaries of the Soul*, p. 91.

23. Carl G. Jung, *Man and His Symbols* (London: Aldus Books, 1964; New York: Dell Publishing Co., 1968), pp. 163–166, 248.

24. Wilder, *Theopoetic*, p. 84.

25. Ibid., pp. 92–93.

26. Wilder, *Early Christian Rhetoric*, p. 129.

27. Wilder, *Jesus' Parables and the War of Myths*, p. 90.

28. Ibid.

29. Wilder, *Theopoetic*, p. 27.

30. Ibid., pp. 27–28.

31. Ibid., p. 29.

Chapter 5: Social Justice Preaching: Some Nuts and Bolts

1. Elizabeth Achtemeier, *Creative Preaching: Finding the Words* (Nashville: Abingdon Press, 1980), p. 24.

2. This is echoed in Fred B. Craddock, *Overhearing the Gospel* (Nashville: Abingdon Press, 1978), pp. 135–137.

3. Milton Crum, Jr., *Manual on Preaching: A New Process of Sermon Development* (Valley Forge, Pa.: Judson Press, 1977); Eugene L. Lowry, *The Homiletical Plot: The Sermon as Narrative Art Form* (Atlanta: John Knox Press, 1980).

4. Michael A. King, "The Castle or the Meadow?" *The Gospel Herald*, Dec. 6, 1983, pp. 848–849.

5. Edward F. Markquart, *Quest for Better Preaching: Resources for Renewal in the Pulpit* (Minneapolis: Augsburg Publishing House, 1985), p. 174.

6. Lowry, *The Homiletical Plot*, p. 24.

7. Craddock, *Overhearing the Gospel*, p. 135.

8. Ernest Best, *From Text to Sermon: Responsible Use of the New Testament in Preaching* (Atlanta: John Knox Press, 1978), p. 92.

9. William D. Thompson, *Preaching Biblically: Exegesis and Interpretation* (Nashville: Abingdon Press, 1981), pp. 14–16.

10. Ibid., pp. 27–35.

11. See such resources as these: Thompson, *Preaching Biblically*, especially pp. 39–77; Reginald H. Fuller, *The Use of the Bible in Preaching* (Philadelphia: Fortress Press, 1981); Leander E. Keck, *The Bible in the Pulpit: The Renewal of Biblical Preaching* (Nashville: Abingdon Press, 1978).

12. Arland J. Hultgren, "Hermeneutical Tendencies in the Three-Year Lectionary," in *Studies in Lutheran Hermeneutics*, ed. by John Reumann et al. (Philadelphia: Fortress Press, 1979), pp. 149–150.

13. Craddock, *Overhearing the Gospel*, p. 90.

14. John Killinger, *Fundamentals of Preaching* (Philadelphia: Fortress Press, 1985), p. 53.

15. Thompson, *Preaching Biblically*, p. 91.

16. Morton T. Kelsey, *The Other Side of Silence: A Guide to Christian Meditation* (Ramsey, N.J.: Paulist/Newman Press, 1976), pp. 21–26.

17. John R. W. Stott, *Between Two Worlds: The Art of Preaching in the Twentieth Century* (Grand Rapids: Wm. B. Eerdmans Publishing Co., 1982); Frederick Buechner, *Telling the Truth: The Gospel as Tragedy, Comedy, and Fairy Tale* (San Francisco: Harper & Row, 1977).

Chapter 6: From Ivory Tower to Life in the Story

1. Frederick Buechner, *The Alphabet of Grace* (New York: Seabury Press, Crossroad Books, 1977), p. 3.

2. Robertson Davies, *The Manticore* (New York: Viking Press, 1972; reprint ed., New York: Penguin Books, 1976), p. 138.

3. C. S. Lewis, *The Lion, the Witch and the Wardrobe* (1950; New York: Macmillan Publishing Co.; Collier Books, 1970).

4. Robert Friedmann, *The Theology of Anabaptism: An Interpretation* (Scottdale, Pa.: Herald Press, 1973), p. 91.

5. Ibid., p. 97.

6. Ben C. Ollenburger, "The Hermeneutics of Obedience," *Essays on Biblical Interpretation: Anabaptist-Mennonite Perspectives*, Text-Reader Series I (Elkhart, Ind.: Institute of Mennonite Studies, 1984), pp. 49, 59.

7. José Míguez-Bonino, *Doing Theology in a Revolutionary Situation* (Philadelphia: Fortress Press, 1975), p. 90.

8. James H. Cone, *God of the Oppressed* (New York: Seabury Press, 1975), pp. 39–61.

9. Fred B. Craddock, *Overhearing the Gospel* (Nashville: Abingdon Press, 1978), p. 88.

10. Ibid.

11. Buechner, *The Alphabet of Grace*, p. 21.

Bibliography

We can suggest here only a few print resources, any one of which is likely to list countless additional resources. Print resources fall into two basic categories: magazines, which provide the most current information in an ongoing way; and books, which tend to be more dated but can provide more breadth and depth.

Among magazines that focus specifically on social issues are *Christianity and Crisis, Engage/Social Action, The Other Side, Sojourners, Transformation,* and *The Witness.* Among magazines that deal with Christian concerns in general but include significant coverage (from a variety of perspectives) of social issues, are *The Christian Century, Christianity Today, Eternity, Reformed Journal,* and a host of denominational magazines. The magazine *Christian Ministry* focuses on the practical side of ministry and frequently features articles and sermons that take into account social issues.

Many of the books cited in the notes contain helpful additional information and their own bibliographies. In addition, we are listing below a sampling of books organized into some of the categories mentioned elsewhere, particularly in chapter 3.

Growing in Multidimensional Understanding

It is difficult to find books in this category that explicitly work at understanding and integrating the various dimensions of issues. Listed below are books that, in one way or another, explore a particular dimension or the integration of several. Taken together, they stimulate multidimensional conceptualization.

Kelly, Thomas R. *A Testament of Devotion.* New York: Harper & Brothers, 1941.
Kelsey, Morton T. *The Other Side of Silence.* Ramsey, N.J.: Paulist/ Newman Press, 1976.

Nouwen, Henri J. M. *Creative Ministry*. Garden City, N.Y.: Doubleday & Co., Image Books, 1978.
Wink, Walter. *Naming the Powers*. Philadelphia: Fortress Press,
1984.

Preaching on Social Issues

Boesak, Allan A. *The Finger of God: Sermons on Faith and Socio-political
Responsibility*. Translated by Peter Randall. Maryknoll, N.Y.:
Orbis Books, 1982.
Coffin, William Sloane. *The Courage to Love*. San Francisco: Harper
& Row, 1982.
Sider, Ronald J., and Darrel J. Brubaker, editors. *Preaching on Peace*.
Philadelphia: Fortress Press, 1982.

A "Reversed" Perspective

Brown, Robert McAfee. *Unexpected News: Reading the Bible with Third
World Eyes*. Philadelphia: Westminster Press, 1984.
Gutiérrez, Gustavo. *A Theology of Liberation: History, Politics and Sal-
vation*. Maryknoll, N.Y.: Orbis Books, 1973.
Kraybill, Donald B. *The Upside-Down Kingdom*. Scottdale, Pa.: Her-
ald Press, 1978.

Abortion

Gorman, Michael J. *Abortion and the Early Church*. Downers Grove,
Ill.: Inter-Varsity Press, 1982.
Harrison, Beverly Wildung. *Our Right to Choose: Toward a New Ethic
of Abortion*. Boston: Beacon Press, 1983.
Noonan, John T., Jr., editor. *The Morality of Abortion: Legal and
Historical Perspectives*. Cambridge, Mass.: Harvard University
Press, 1970.
Sider, Ronald J. *Completely Pro-Life*. Downers Grove, Ill.: Inter-
Varsity Press, 1987.
Young, Curt. *The Least of These*. Chicago: Moody Press, 1983.

Economic Justice

Nelson, Jack A. *Hunger for Justice: The Politics of Food and Faith*.
Maryknoll, N.Y.: Orbis Books, 1980.
Schwartz-Nobel, Loretta. *Starving in the Shadow of Plenty*. New York:
G. P. Putnam's Sons, 1981.
Sider, Ronald J. *Rich Christians in an Age of Hunger*. Second edition.
Downers Grove, Ill.: Inter-Varsity Press, 1984.

Human Rights

Boesak, Allan Aubrey. *Walking on Thorns: The Call to Christian Obedience*. Grand Rapids: Wm. B. Eerdmans Publishing Co., 1984.

Ellis, Carl F., Jr. *Beyond Liberation*. Downers Grove, Ill.: Inter-Varsity Press, 1983.

Tutu, Desmond. *Hope and Suffering*. Grand Rapids: Wm. B. Eerdmans Publishing Co., 1984.

The Earth

Carmody, John. *Ecology and Religion: Toward a New Christian Theology of Nature*. New York: Paulist Press, 1983.

Granberg-Michaelson, Wesley. *A Worldly Spirituality: The Call to Redeem Life on Earth*. San Francisco: Harper & Row, 1984.

Owens, Virginia Stem. *And the Trees Clap Their Hands: Faith, Perception, and the New Physics*. Grand Rapids: Wm. B. Eerdmans Publishing Co., 1983.

Santmire, H. Paul. *The Travail of Nature: The Ambiguous Ecological Promise of Christian Theology*. Philadelphia: Fortress Press, 1985.

Wilkinson, Loren, editor. *Earthkeeping: Christian Stewardship of Natural Resources*. Grand Rapids: Wm. B. Eerdmans Publishing Co., 1980.

War and Violence

Bainton, Roland. *Christian Attitudes Toward War and Peace*. Nashville: Abingdon Press, 1960.

Sider, Ronald J., and Richard K. Taylor. *Nuclear Holocaust and Christian Hope*. Downers Grove, Ill.: Inter-Varsity Press, 1982.

Wallis, Jim, editor. *Waging Peace: A Handbook for the Struggle Against Nuclear Arms*. San Francisco: Harper & Row, 1982.

Social Issues and Christian Community

Geaney, Dennis J. *The Prophetic Parish: A Center for Peace and Justice*. Minneapolis: Winston Press, 1983.

Hauerwas, Stanley. *A Community of Character: Toward a Constructive Christian Social Ethic*. Notre Dame, Ind.: University of Notre Dame Press, 1981.

Sine, Tom. *The Mustard Seed Conspiracy*. Waco, Tex.: Word Books, 1981.

Lincoln Christian College

7705

251
S;5